The Clouds
and
The Pot of Gold

Crofts Classics

GENERAL EDITORS

Samuel H. Beer, *Harvard University*

O. B. Hardison, Jr., *Georgetown University*

TWO CLASSICAL COMEDIES

The Clouds
by *ARISTOPHANES*
and
The Pot of Gold
by *PLAUTUS*

TRANSLATED AND EDITED BY

Peter D. Arnott

TUFTS UNIVERSITY

Harlan Davidson, Inc.
Arlington Heights, Illinois 60004

Library of Congress Cataloging-in-Publication Data

Two classical comedies.

    (Crofts classics)
    Reprint. Originally published: New York: Appleton-Century-Crofts, 1967.
    Bibliography: p.
    Contents: The clouds / by Aristophanes—The pot of gold / by Plautus.
    1. Classical drama (Comedy)—Translations into English. 2. English drama (Comedy)—Translations from classical languages. I. Arnott, Peter D. II. Aristophanes. Clouds. English. 1986. III. Plautus, Titus Maccius. Pot of gold. English, 1986.
PA3629.T86   1986b   882'.01'08   86-2211
ISBN 0-88295-005-3 (pbk.)

Manufactured in the United States of America
92 91 90 89 88 MG 9 10 11 12 13

INTRODUCTION

ARISTOPHANES AND THE CLOUDS

THE CLOUDS belongs to the *genre* known as Old Comedy, the distinctive Greek comic form of the fifth century B.C. For us, because of the selective processes of literary survival, Old Comedy and Aristophanes are virtually synonymous. Although a multitude of fragments have been preserved, we have no complete plays by any other author from this important period. It is a form that, for modern audiences and readers, contains some unusual and occasionally puzzling features. They are puzzling, however, only because modern ideas of comedy derive from a later period, finding their source in the sort of play that Plautus wrote rather than in Aristophanes. Once we make the necessary mental adjustment Aristophanes' comedies may be seen as a natural outgrowth of the theater and social conditions of his time.

Greek comedy, like Greek tragedy, seems to have originated in community festivals and choral revels, and the basic ingredients are the same in each case—a chorus that can both act as narrator or commentator and take an important part in the action, and a limited number of actors who may each take several roles in the course of one play. Tragedy develops as a fairly rigid alternation of choral song and acted scenes. In comedy the pattern is looser. This is probably due to the comparatively late date at which comedy won official recognition and was admitted to the dramatic festivals. It had less time to acquire rules and traditions, and so developed in a more flexible and uninhibited manner. In comedy the chorus may have immense importance in some parts of the play and be practically ignored at others. The dramatist is free to manipulate the various components of his comedy as the mood takes him. In tragedy the dramatist was limited by expediency and convention to a fairly small repertoire of

well-known stories. In comedy the writer invented his own
plots, with the various advantages and liabilities that this
implies.

Within this generally loose structure there appear, in
the plays of Aristophanes, certain recurrent features. The
comedies normally end with a revel (*kōmos*)—sometimes,
more specifically, a marriage—or with a riotous assembly,
as in *The Clouds,* where Strepsiades drives Socrates and
the students from their blazing home. The plays usually
contain a set debate (*agon*) inserted into the framework
of the play. In *The Clouds* we have, in fact, two such
debates. The first is staged by Socrates in his Academy
as part of Pheidippides' education and is delivered by
characters representing True and False Logic. The second, reminiscent of the first in both pattern and language,
takes place between Strepsiades and Pheidippides himself,
with the son proving by perverted logic that it is right
and just for him to beat his own father. Another regular
feature of Aristophanic comedy is the lengthy passage
(*parabasis*) where the chorus addresses the audience
directly, either in or out of character, and comments on
some matter of topical importance or something in which
the poet himself feels a concern. In this comedy the
parabasis is complicated by the play's revision. The long
passage criticising the audience's judgement (vv. 561ff.)
was clearly composed after the failure of the first performance. The remainder must belong to the original
version.

These three recurring features, *kōmos, agon* and
parabasis, have been traced back by some scholars to a
form of predramatic religious ritual. It is argued that they
stem from some early type of "seasonal combat" in which
a character representing Spring fought with another representing Winter, or the New Year with the Old, and
finally defeated him—hence, with the element of physical
violence minimized, the *agon*—and which ended with the
enactment of a "sacred marriage" to bring fertility to the
fields—hence the *kōmos.* According to this theory the
parabasis is seen as one half of an original choral *agon*
in which the chorus itself would divide and take sides to
debate some important issue. There are cases in Aristophanes where this type of choral division occurs, for

example in *Lysistrata*, where the old men are matched against the old women.

Such theories are in the last analysis unprovable, and it is doubtful whether they are necessary. Each of the above-mentioned features is explicable in terms of Aristophanes' theater and the conditions in which he had to work. In the open, uncurtained and naturally illuminated theater for which Aristophanes wrote, some sort of lavish song-and-dance spectacle was almost a necessity for the playwright if he wanted his comedy to have an effective finale. Once we see the plays as musical comedies—which they were; it is our misfortune that the music has been lost—the *kōmos* no longer seems extraordinary. Given that the author already has a chorus at his disposal, a dance or procession is the obvious way of ending the play on a high note and at the same time clearing the stage of characters. The *kōmos* performs a natural function and needs no special explanation. By the same token the *agon* and *parabasis* may be seen as evolving naturally from the tastes and habits of the people. Greeks loved debate. Most of Aristophanes' audience spent the greater part of their time in the debates, meetings and assemblies through which the democracy functioned. The techniques of rhetoric would have been far more familiar to them than they are to us, and when Aristophanes employs debate form to present an argument or make a point he is doing no more than employing a pattern to which he knows his audience is already attuned. In the same way the later medieval playwrights utilized the sermon form for their dramas, working in terms with which their audiences were already familiar. As for the *parabasis*, we only find it odd because our theater has, for the most part, lost the facility of direct address to the audience that the Greeks enjoyed. In the Greek theater the audience surrounded the action and was separated from it neither by any structural barrier nor by light. The spectators were one with the performance that evolved in their midst, and in such circumstances it is natural for the writer to recognize their presence and address them directly. The reader will notice many occasions outside the *parabasis* where this type of direct address is employed; the *parabasis* itself is no more than a temporary heightening of a tendency already strongly present. When such things happen in our own theater the effect tends to be either one of shock—as when the Knights address the audience in *Murder in the Cathedral*—or archness, as is the case so frequently in the plays of Thornton Wilder. We have been conditioned by four hundred years of the proscenium stage, which the Greeks never knew.

In its subject matter Old Comedy could be wickedly topical. Aristophanes was free to discourse, virtually without restraint, on men and matters of note. The Greeks knew few laws of libel or slander. Athens, by modern standards, was a small town, and as in all small towns the best jokes were personal jokes; everyone knew everyone, and the smallest personal references would have been understood and appreciated. In such an atmosphere any prominent man, in whatever field, would naturally suggest himself as a target. In *The Clouds* the principal butt is one of the greatest Athenians, the philosopher Socrates, who was living and teaching when the play was written and who, according to tradition, was in the audience to see himself mocked. He was a target that Aristophanes could hardly have avoided even if he wanted to. His odd personal appearance, his unorthodox opinions and his irregular way of life would have singled him out for attention. We who come to Socrates by way of Plato and with the hindsight of his martyrdom must with the best will in the world view this portrayal with a sense of outrage. Once again, we have to make a mental readjustment. The question of whether Aristophanes is being fair to Socrates is irrelevant. Of course he is not. The Socrates of the play is a travesty of the Socrates of actuality, the Socrates we may perceive through Plato's dialogues and Xenophon's more pedestrian biography. (It is important, however, to remember that these writers may have been biased in one direction as much as Aristophanes was in the other.) The comic Socrates is really little more than that familiar theatrical caricature, the Learned Man, the Comic Professor, embellished with such humor as contemporary fashion would suggest. Aristophanes was not alone in mining this comic vein; others had written their Socrates plays, and from the little we know of them it would seem they were developed along the same lines. Aristophanes' Socrates is not made the mouthpiece of any specific philosophy; as a portrait, the caricature is not even consistent with itself. He is given some traits associated with the early Ionian scientific philosophers—it is thus that we first hear of him, through his student, conducting various pseudo-scientific experiments. At other parts of the play he appears as a mystic, using devices associated with the Orphic and other cults. Preeminently, however, he is what the real Socrates never was, a teacher of rhetoric and an exponent of sophistry in its most pernicious aspects.

The sophists (the name means "practitioners of wisdom," and only later acquired its derogatory connotation) were a recent phenomenon in Greece. They were itinerant teachers, conducting classes for a fee—often a large one —and both responding to and helping to create the new intellectual climate. By the middle of the fifth century men were beginning to turn away from the established religion and assert the impossibility of discovering man's relationship to the gods, or even of the existence of such gods. The focus of investigation narrowed; men turned to other, more restricted but more immediately fruitful fields of speculation, concentrating on what they could measure and evaluate, what was close at hand. Interest was now increasingly in humanistic studies, in political science and ethics, in the art of successful living and the branches of learning that would aid worldly success; in short, in man himself, and no longer in man in relation to his gods. The sophists taught what men wished to know. Several of them were admirable and disinterested philosophers; others were charlatans, prepared to offer easy formulae for success, and the most obvious avenue to such success in Greek public life, and therefore the subject most frequently taught by the sophists, was rhetoric. Athens, always litigious and argumentative, took the new teaching to its heart. This is what is mirrored in the play. Strepsiades seeks rhetorical ability to confound his creditors, and Socrates is represented as the prototypical sophist who professes to instruct him.

The Learned Man of modern popular comedy tends to be a nuclear physicist or a psychiatrist. In Aristophanes he is a sophistic rhetorician. In both cases the caricature is dictated by prevailing fashion. Where modern comedy can only borrow the white hair and spectacles of an Einstein, Aristophanes, less restricted, can select a real personage to serve as a peg for his caricature, and he chooses to employ a philosopher everyone would have heard of and who is already sufficiently eccentric to be the butt of others' jokes. This is not a portrait of Socrates as he was, but it may very well be a portrait of Socrates as the Athenian-in-the-street imagined him when he bothered to think seriously about him at all. We tend to overestimate the intelligence of the Athenian public and their interest in such matters as philosophy. We need to remind ourselves constantly that not every citizen of Athens was a Plato, or even a Xenophon; this is proved by the fact that they chose to execute Socrates. To his disciples Socrates was a genius, and we perforce see him with this aura. The average Athenian probably thought of Socrates as an eccentric fat man who had chosen to give up a respectable profession and spent his time in the streets asking extraordinary questions. We cannot deduce anything from the play as to what Aristophanes' true feelings for Socrates were—he is represented later by Plato as being on good terms with him—but once again the question is irrelevant. If there is true criticism in the play at all it is of the times and not of the man. In the confrontation between the old way of life and the new, with its focus here in the *agon* between True and False Logic, Aristophanes shows himself sensitive to the changing complexion of his city; to the acceptance of new codes, new standards, a new way of life which contrasted radically with those that had obtained earlier when different men had been in control and Athens had been unperturbed by serious threat of war. Again, one cannot safely make any deductions about what Aristophanes' own views were. He is a popular dramatist, and his plays tend to represent popular viewpoints. Those developed here—that the old times were best, and that modern youth was going to the dogs— are consistently popular and universal. Substitute racing cars for racing chariots, and Zen for sophistry, and the portrait of Pheidippides would seem totally modern. Certainly there is much in the sophistic movement that Aristophanes would have liked. He would have been sympathetic to the fresh, critical spirit that manifested itself in the best sophistic teachers. It would be wrong, however, to represent him as a sermonizer or a propagandist for any movement. With him the joke is the important thing, and to the immediate joke all considerations of logic, consistency and fair-mindedness must be sacrificed.

The Athenian plays were performed competitively, and Aristophanes shows himself aware of the presence of the judges. He wants to win first prize, and says so. Nonetheless he failed. Why, we can only guess. The most probable surmise is that his humor was originally too erudite for the public taste; he may have attempted a parody of Socrates which came nearer the truth, and was *ipso facto* above the heads of the multitude. The version we have, and the one that is translated here, is a composite version representing the greater part of the original text with some revisions. We do not know when these revisions were made, or if Aristophanes ever had the revised text performed. We do not even know, except in the obvious case of the *parabasis*, what the revisions were. An ancient commentator tells us that two other portions of the play suffered major changes, namely, the debate between True and False Logic and the finale. Conjectures have been made in plenty, but certainty is impossible.

For the translator the play presents several striking problems. In all his plays Aristophanes uses puns—they are one of his favorite forms of humor—but in none are the puns so crucial to the meaning as they are here. In a comedy that treats of ambiguity and deception the language is ambiguous and deceptive to suit. Furthermore, the more important puns are virtually untranslatable as they stand. To retain intelligibility, let alone humor, some reasonable alternative has to be found which will retain the spirit of the Greek while forfeiting the letter. Therefore in several instances the text given here does not represent what the Greek actually says. Examples are Strepsiades' confusion over musical terminology (vv. 722-7) and masculine and feminine nouns (vv. 733-41). The latter joke translates well enough into French, which recognizes genders, but not into English, which has none. In cases where important departures have been made from the text the literal meaning of the original has been explained in footnotes.

PLAUTUS AND THE POT OF GOLD

By the end of the fifth century much had happened to change the pattern of Greek comedy and the role of the theater in Greek society. First came the disastrous consequences of the war years. The type of comedy to which *The Clouds* belongs could flourish only in a state that felt itself secure from without, and so could tolerate open criticism from within. Aristophanes criticizes politicians, generals and other leaders of state with the same gleeful abandon, and the same utter disregard for fair play, that he shows for the philosophers. The reader will note that even in the generally non-political *Clouds* many disrespectful things are said about politicians. A weakened state could no longer allow such criticism, and a stricter censorship begins to operate. Aristophanes' later plays show a turning away from the topicality and pungent satire that marked his earlier work; the themes become deliberately innocuous, and his last play, *Wealth* (classed as Middle, i.e. transitional, Comedy) is nothing more than a gentle, impersonal allegory. Another important change was the expansion and secularization of theatrical activity. For the greater part of the fifth century, the theater had been connected specifically with worship. Plays were given at festival time only, were restricted to short periods each year and formed part of a collective act of religious observance. In the fourth century this was no longer true. The commercial possibilities of theater were accepted and exploited. Plays were now performed by professional companies operating independently of the major festivals and giving shows wherever and whenever they could find an audience. In such a situation Aristophanic comedy was no longer useful. Athenian jokes were not funny outside Athens. The new audiences demanded plays that they could understand, and as Greek influences expanded eastward and Alexander's armies pressed towards India, taking Greek culture in their train, the theater found itself compelled to investigate other types of comedy. Something was needed that would be cosmopolitan in its appeal and generalized in its humor, the sort of comedy that could be played to any audience anywhere in the world provided only that it spoke Greek. In practical terms this implies concentration on domestic situations and characters, and later Greek comedy (New Comedy) draws most of its plots from these sources. Characters become stereotyped into easily recognizable molds. Plots employ the same standard formulae with minor variations—romantic love, mistaken identity, the long-lost child. In plays of this sort, characterization tends to become shallow and plots unimaginative: we are shown a range of familiar types and asked to observe what happens when some arbitrary circumstance brings them into conflict—for *tyche*, luck, chance or coincidence, is the motivating factor in these Hellenistic comedies, and indeed was the nearest thing to a deity that many of this time would have recognized. The dramatist could best display his skill in the mechanics of plot construction and in the ingenious dovetailing of characters, themes and incidents.

Hardly anything of the Greek New Comedies has survived for us to read. We know them principally through the imitations and translations made by Roman writers. When Rome expanded its influence throughout Italy the first important culture with which it came into contact was Greek, represented by the Greek colonies in the South. Here stood cities that had been thriving when Rome was only a primitive village, that had maintained close contact with the motherland and served to transmit Greek art and letters to Italian soil. Rome achieved military supremacy before it had attained cultural independence. Confronted with the polished works of a long-established and still flourishing culture, it took them over wholesale. Roman plays, like much of the rest of Roman culture, are fundamentally Greek works translated and adapted. Roman writers found it easier to take Greek plots than to invent new ones. It was a time-saving fashion. Roman theater was completely commercial, and the dramatist, who sold his play outright and earned no royalties, was forced to produce a constant flow of material if he wished to survive. Another consequence of this commercialization was the fall in status of the theater and those connected with it. In Greece the theater had been an honorable institution, borrowing the odor of sanctity and amateur in the finest sense of the world. In Rome

theater was for amusement only, and the writer, who
earned his living from his pen, was forced to write down
to the popular level of comprehension.

Titus Maccius Plautus—the name has theatrical con-
notations—was the most popular of the Roman comic
writers. Twenty-one of his plays have survived for us, but
he must have written more than these; other playwrights
and theater managers were happy to plagiarize his work
and use his name on their bills, for a play by Plautus
would always draw a crowd. Although he inserts occa-
sional Roman descriptions and topicalities to appeal to
his own audience, Plautus' works are still, substantially,
Greek New Comedies translated into Latin. *The Pot of
Gold* (*Aulularia*) is no exception. The plot employs the
customary formulae: the love affair with complications,
the secrets, the eventual discoveries. The characters fall
into the same familiar categories: the angry old man
(Euclio), the kindly old man (Megadorus), the young
lover (Lyconides), and the various comic slaves. It is
fitting that the prologue should be spoken by the Household God, for the spirit of domesticity presides over New
and Roman Comedy; the plays regularly concern themselves with domestic affairs and relationships. What gives
this play extra appeal, however, is the fact that the characters do not remain wholly within their stereotypes.
Euclio, though miserly, is something else besides a miser.
Plautus gives him moments of considerable dignity and
self-respect. The speech in which he debates the pro-
priety of a marriage-alliance with the rich Megadorus
(vv. 287ff.) reveals the sturdy common sense and in-
stinct for order which was one of the finest characteristics
of the Roman Republic. This can perhaps best be seen by
comparing the play with its famous French imitation,
Molière's *L'Avare* (*The Miser*). Here most of the incidents
and characters are drawn directly from Plautus, but Har-
pagon, Molière's counterpart of Euclio, is more nearly a
pure miser and is short of the redeeming qualities that
make Euclio interesting. It is true that in Plautus all the
characters tend to be preoccupied with their own affairs—
Euclio with his money, Lyconides with his love affair, the
slaves with their cooking—and that the humor comes
when these individual interests are brought into conflict,

but these preoccupations are often tempered with more altruistic reasoning, as in the case of Euclio and as in Megadorus' theories on marriage and the well-being of the state.

Plautus was a popular playwright, and popular plays tend to suffer more damage than unpopular ones; they are more frequently copied, passed from hand to hand, emended and rearranged to suit the tastes of individual performers. The manuscript of *The Pot of Gold* as it has come down to us presents several serious problems. There is, for instance, obvious confusion in the names of the slaves and the attribution of parts to each. In the text as it stands both the slave of Megadorus who supervises the dinner preparations (vv. 364ff.) and the slave of Lyconides who comes to spy out the land for his master (vv. 728ff.) are called Strobilus. They cannot be the same person, and it is impossible that in a complex plot of this nature Plautus would have given two characters the same name. It has been suggested that in the original both names might have begun with the same letters (e.g. Strobilus and Strolus) so that both would have been abbreviated to STR-, thus initiating the confusion. Then there is the strange case of Pythodicus, who in the Latin emerges from nowhere, speaks one speech (vv. 461ff.) and vanishes. Something had to be done. The present version follows the example of some earlier editions in assigning the name Pythodicus to Megadorus' slave, and Strobilus to Lyconides' slave. The name Strobilus (Greek *strobilos*, spinning top) seems better suited to the volatile character who steals the pot, while Pythodicus, with its pontifical overtones, seems more appropriate to the officious person who arranges the banquet. These identifications are far from certain, and there are several objections that can be made to them. Nevertheless, for the sake of simplicity at least, this arrangement has something to commend it.

More serious is the question of how the play ends. In our Latin texts the play breaks off abruptly after the disclosure by Strobilus that he has stolen the gold (v. 1038 in this version; the break is indicated in the text.) For the sake of completeness, and to aid those who may wish to perform the play, an original ending has been added.

Plautus and his commentators in fact offer some guide-lines. The second, acrostic Argument, written presumably by someone who had access to the complete text, indicates that Lyconides reveals the theft and wins his bride, and more importantly, that Euclio gives up the pot of gold. This is supported by one fragmentary line that has been displaced from the text and is here included as v. 1109. Euclio here seems to indicate that he is giving his treasure away. The present version, then, tries to wind the play up plausibly and with reasonable brevity, Plautus' own endings being often perfunctory, to say the least. The final appeal for applause is, of course, mandatory in Roman comedy.

Neither in *The Clouds* nor in *The Pot of Gold* does the original text contain stage directions. They are almost nonexistent in ancient drama. In most cases sufficient indication of movement and business is given by the text itself. In these translations indications have been given of principal exits and entrances and occasionally a direction has been added to clarify the meaning of an obscure line.

PRINCIPAL DATES IN THE LIFE
OF ARISTOPHANES

c.450 B.C.	Birth of Aristophanes
431	Outbreak of war between Athens and Sparta
427	Production of first play, *Daitales* ("The Banqueters")—no longer extant.
426	Production of *The Babylonians*, attacking the demagogue Cleon—no longer extant.
425	*The Acharnians*
424	*The Knights*
423	Production of *The Clouds*.
422	*The Wasps*
421	*The Peace*
414	*The Birds*
411	*Lysistrata*
	Thesmophoriazousae ("Mother's Day")
405	*The Frogs*
404	End of Peloponnesian War; Athens yields to Sparta.
399	Execution of Socrates
391	*Ecclesiazousae* (*Parliament of Women*)
388	*Plutus* ("Wealth")
c.385	Death of Aristophanes

PRINCIPAL DATES IN THE LIFE OF PLAUTUS

c.251 B.C.	Birth of Plautus
after 206	Production of *Miles Goriosus* ("*Captain Cock-sure*")
200	Production of *Stichus*
191	Production of *Pseudolus*
184	Death of Plautus

Information on Plautus' life is scanty, and the above dates are all that can be inferred with any degree of certainty. Tradition asserts that he was born at Sarsina, in Umbria, central Italy; that he worked in the theater, acquired money, lost it and was reduced to working in a flour mill; that he there began to write plays, and soon became a highly popular dramatist. It is uncertain how much of this is fact and how much unsupported guesswork drawn from the contents of the plays themselves. He was frequently imitated, and soon after his death there was already confusion over the works attributed to him. We now possess 21 plays by him, but he certainly wrote more than this. No certain date can be given to *The Pot of Gold*.

THE CLOUDS

Aristophanes

CHARACTERS

STREPSIADES, *an old countryman, now resident in Athens.*

PHEIDIPPIDES, *his son, an extravagant and fashionable young man.*

SLAVE of STREPSIADES

STUDENTS of SOCRATES' *Academy.*

SOCRATES, *a philosopher.*

CHORUS of CLOUDS

TRUE LOGIC

FALSE LOGIC

PASIAS, *a moneylender.*

AMYNIAS, *another moneylender.*

WITNESS, *who accompanies* PASIAS.

Other slaves of STREPSIADES' *household.*

The setting is Athens. Two houses are represented, one belonging to STREPSIADES *and the other to* SOCRATES.

THE CLOUDS

[*The house of* STREPSIADES. *It is just before dawn.* STREP-
SIADES *and* PHEIDIPPIDES *are in bed, the former wide awake
and the latter tossing and muttering in his sleep. A slave is
asleep nearby.*]

STREPSIADES. Hey ho!
Good god almighty, how these nights go on
And on, and on . . . won't daylight ever come?
I heard the cock crow hours ago, and here's
The help, still snoring. Things aren't what they used to be.
War, there are lots of reasons why I'd like
To see the end of you: I can't so much
As raise a hand against my servants now.
[*gesturing towards* PHEIDIPPIDES]
And then young hopeful here: he never
Opens his eyes all night, just rolls himself
In half a dozen coverlets, and makes   10
A bad smell in the bed. All right, let's pull
The bedclothes round my ears again, and snore . . .

[*He tries unsuccessfully to sleep. After a brief pause he
uncovers himself again.*]

Not a hope. I'm being eaten up alive
By debts and feed-bills and extravagance.
And it's all his fault. My son. He gets himself
A horsey haircut, joins the hunting set,
Keeps his carriage and pair, and not content with that
Rides horseback in his sleep. It's killing me.
It's that time of the month again, the bills
Are pouring in.
[*calling to the slave*] Give me some light, there, boy,   20

5 **War** between Athens and Sparta, in progress at the time of
the play   7 **against my servants** ill-treated slaves would desert
to the Spartan side

3

And bring me my accounts, so I can see
How many people I owe money to
And reckon up the payments due. Here goes.

[*The slave brings a lamp and the account book.* STREP-
SIADES *reads.*]

Now, what's the damage? Pasias, five hundred.
Five hundred? Pasias? What for? What did I do
With that? I bought a gelding?
They should have gelded me before I bought it.

    PHEIDIPPIDES. [*talking in his sleep*] Hey, Philon, that's
      against the rules! You're cutting in!

    STREPS. [*to the audience*] You hear that? That's what's
      been the ruin of me.

He even thinks of horses in his sleep.

    PHEID. [*as before*] How many times round for the Mili-
30   tary Handicap?

    STREPS. You've ridden me around a time or two.

[*turning back to his accounts*] Tell me the worst. Who's
    after Pasias?

Amynias, two fifty for a chariot
And a pair of wheels.

    PHEID. [*as before*] Roll my horse and stable him.

    STREPS. You've rolled me for everything I have.

The courts have got me on the run, and people
Are saying that they'll take my goods in payment.

    PHEID. [*waking up*] Father, is there anything upsetting
     you?

40 You've been tossing and turning all night long!

    STREPS. It's just that every time I try to settle
Down, I feel the pinch.

    PHEID.   Well, be a good chap

And let me get some sleep. [*He lies down again.*]

    STREPS.   Yes, go to sleep!

But I can promise you one thing, these debts
Will fall on your head one day. Oh,
I hope she rots in hell, that matchmaker
Who put me up to marrying your mother.
I had a little farm, and I was happy
As the day was long—no worries and no housework,

42 **pinch** a pun: from poverty and from the bedbugs

No flies in the ointment, olives for the picking,   50
My sheepfolds full, my beehives brimming over—
And then I had to marry her. Her father's
Brother was a Megacles, and so was his . . .
A hick like me, and her a city girl
Who'd been raised soft. Did she look down her nose
At everybody! Let me tell you, snobbery
Was her middle name. And that's the girl I married
And took to bed. I smelt of musty winecasks,
Figs drying in the sun, and fullness of fine fleeces,
And she of smart boutiques, exotic perfume,   60
Tongue-kisses and high living, dinner parties,
And love's young dream, and kiss-me-quick. I must say,
    though,
She wasn't idle. On the contrary,
She was always darning. I'd hold up my cloak
For her to see, and preach a sermon on it:
"With you it's darn the housework, darn expense,
Darn everything!"
    SLAVE.   The lamp's run out of oil.
    STREPS. Why did you light that one? That's no lamp,
It's a sponge. Come here and take your punishment.
    SLAVE. Why do you want to punish me?
    STREPS.   Because   70
You put one of the thick wicks in it. [beating him] Well,
In good time there was born this son of mine
To me and my good woman, and at once
We started fighting over what to christen him.
It was her idea to call him something -hippus,
Xanthippus, or Charippus, or Callippides.
I wanted him Pheidonides for his grandad.
We argued for a bit, and in the end
We comprised, and named the boy Pheidippides.
She used to take the lad and fill his head   80
With nonsense, telling him "One day you'll be
Grown up, and drive down town in the parade

53 **Megacles** of the Alcmaeonid family, one of the most illustrious and aristocratic houses in Athens   75 **-hippus** "horse," an aristocratic suffix   77 **Pheidonides for his grandad** Greek boys were commonly named after their grandparents; the name means "sparing"

Like Megacles in purple," and I said
"One day you'll drive your goats down from the ridge
Dressed in a leather jerkin like your father."
I might as well have saved my breath. On his account
I'm all at sea, I've caught the hand-to-mouth disease.
All night I've racked my brains to find a way
And I've struck one, a superspecial highway—
90 If I can win him over to it, I'll be saved.
First wake him up, though. How can I do that
Without disturbing him? [*waking him*] Pheidippides!
Yoohoo, Pheidippides!

    PHEID. [*waking*]   What's the matter now?

    STREPS. You may shake me by the hand. Give me a kiss.

    PHEID. [*complying*] All right. Let's have it.

    STREPS.   Do you love your father?

    PHEID. By Poseidon, god of horses, yes I do.

    STREPS. Don't mention anything to do with horses!
That's the god who's been the ruin of me.
But if you really love me from the bottom of your heart
Do as I tell you, son.

100   PHEID.   Go on. Do what?

    STREPS. It's later than you think. Shake off your present
    habits
And go and get yourself the education
That I'll prescribe for you.

    PHEID.   All right, let's hear it.

    STREPS. You promise, then?

    PHEID.   All right, by . . . yes, I promise.

    STREPS. [*pointing*] Now look in this direction. Can you
    see
The little house there with the gate in front?

    PHEID. I see it all right. But what the devil is it?

    STREPS. That's Highbrow Hall, the hallowed seat of
    learning.
Do you know what? The faculty there say
110 That space is a hotbox, and we're the coals inside.

96 **Poseidon** in his major aspect god of oceans, but also associated with certain animals, notably horse and bull   110 **hotbox** currently fashionable scientific jargon. The philosopher Hippo had used this image to describe the circumambient atmosphere; by a comic extension of the idea Aristophanes asserts that if the atmosphere is a sort of oven, men must be the charcoal inside it

They'll give you lessons, if you pay their fees,
In how to make men believe anything you say,
Whether it's true or not.
    PHEID.   Who are these people?
    STREPS. I can't remember what they're called exactly,
But they can split hairs with the best of them.
    PHEID. Oh, them! I know *them*—they're a no-good
    crowd
Who don't believe in wearing shoes or taking
Exercise; there's not an honest man among them.
That goddamn Socrates is one, and Chaerephon—
    STREPS. I won't hear any more. That's baby talk.   120
But if you want to put a crust into
Your father's mouth, cut out the horses and join them.
    PHEID. I wouldn't be seen dead among that lot
For a whole stable full of thoroughbreds.
    STREPS. Please, son whom I love best in all the world,
Go take some lessons from them.
    PHEID.   What sort of lessons?
    STREPS. The story is, they have two sorts of argument,
The better one, whichever that is, and the worse.
They say that they can take the second one,
The worse, that is, and teach it to prevaricate   130
So it will win out. So do this for me,
Learn how to argue your way out of things,
And all the debts that I've run up on your account—
I'll never have to pay a cent to anyone.
    PHEID. I couldn't do it. I'd never have the nerve
To look my fine friends in the Jockey Club
In the face, if I went round looking like a corpse.
    STREPS. God's sakes! You've had your last meal out of
    me.
You and your four-in-hand and thoroughbreds,
Never darken my door again. To hell with you.   140
    PHEID. Well, uncle Megacles won't see me go
Without a horse. I'm off. That's what I think of you.
                         [*Exit.*]

111 **fees** one conspicuous difference between the stage Socrates
and his living counterpart, who charged nothing for his teaching
117 **shoes** a more accurate description: Socrates liked to go
barefoot 119 **Chaerephon** disciple of Socrates, apparently of
cadaverous appearance: see v. 550

STREPS. I may be down, but I'm not out, not yet!
I'll say a prayer, walk down to Highbrow Hall
And register myself!

[*He walks slowly to the door of* SOCRATES' *Academy.*]

But I'm way over age,
Slow, muddleminded. What hope have I of learning
How to split hairs and chop logic? Well, here goes.
What am I waiting for? [*knocking*] Knock on the door.
Hey boy! Yoohoo!

STUDENT. [*within*] Hell! Who's that knocking?

150   STREPS. Strepsiades from out of town. My father's name
Was Pheidon.

STUDENT. [*opening the door*] You must be some kind
    of idiot
To come here kicking on the door like that.
Don't you have any manners? I was pregnant
With thought, and it's miscarried, all because of you.

STREPS. Don't be angry, I'm a country boy.
But tell me what it was I made miscarry.

STUDENT. Against the rules. We mustn't tell outsiders.

STREPS. There isn't any problem then. I've come
To Highbrow Hall to register, so tell me.

160   STUDENT. All right, but you must swear to keep it quiet.
A while back Socrates was asking Chaerephon
How many of its feet a flea could jump.
You see, one had bitten Chaerephon over his eyebrow
And jumped from there to Socrates' cranium.

STREPS. How did he measure it?

STUDENT.   You never heard
Anything so clever. He melted down some wax,
Caught the flea and dipped its feet in it,
And when it cooled, it stood there wearing slippers!
He took them off and measured out the distance.

170   STREPS. Good god almighty, what an intellect!

STUDENT. What would you say if I told you something
    else
That Socrates thought up himself?

STREPS.   Well, tell me.

STUDENT. Chaerephon asked him in his acid way
"Tell me, do mosquitoes hum

Through the mouth or through the bum?"
   STREPS. Mosquitoes, eh? What did he say to that?
   STUDENT. He argued that the guts of a mosquito
Are small bore. Through this minuscule diameter
Air builds up pressure and seeks outlet at the tail.
The anus is appended to the windpipe. When   180
The wind-force increases, the result is humming.
   STREPS. So mosquitoes can play fanfares on their bot-
     toms!
The man's a genius. He knows physics from
The bottom up. He could go into court
And come out free as air, knowing all he knows
About mosquitoes' guts.
   STUDENT.   A day or two ago
We were deprived of a momentous thought
On account of a lizard.
   STREPS.   Tell me all about it.
   STUDENT. He was investigating the trajectories
And orbits of the moon. There was a lizard on   190
The roof, and while he stood there stargazing
The lizard's droppings fell into his mouth.
   STREPS. I like that. Hey, he really fouled him up.
   STUDENT. Then yesterday, the cupboard was bare—
   STREPS. Clean out of oatmeal, eh? How did he
Work his way out of that situation?
   STUDENT. He sprinkled a layer of ashes on the table,
Bent a skewer double, held it like a pair
Of compasses, and hooked a singlet from the locker room!
   STREPS. Move over, Thales, you've got competition.   200
Do me a favor. Open Highbrow Hall.
Don't keep me in suspense. Let me see Socrates.
I want to go to school. Open the door!

[*The* STUDENT *opens the door, and other students are re-
    vealed engaged in various scholarly pursuits.*]

189 **He was investigating** echo of a more famous story about
the philosopher Thales (see v. 200n.) who fell into a well
while staring at the stars   200 **Thales** early scientific philosopher of Miletus in Asia Minor, concerned with discovering
the material origin of the universe, highly regarded in later
Greek tradition and included in the list of Greek wise men

Hey, what in the world are these supposed to be?

STUDENT. Why so surprised? What do you think they are?

STREPS. They're Spartans, straight out of a prison camp.

What are they looking on the ground for?

STUDENT.   It's a research Project in geology.

STREPS.   Oh, are they hunting truffles?

[*to the students*] Don't worry, you can save yourselves the bother.

210 I'll tell you where the best and biggest grow.

[*pointing to more students*]

Look at these, bent double! What are they working at?

STUDENT. They're down there raising hell.

STREPS.   Then what's His bottom doing pointing to the sky?

STUDENT. It's taking private lessons in astronomy.

[*to the students*] Come along, in you go, before He catches you.

STREPS. Not just yet! Let them stay a little longer So I can tell them what's on my mind—

STUDENT. No, it's against the rules. They mustn't stay In the open air for too long at a time.

STREPS. [*inspecting more students and equipment*]

220 And what's all this about, for heaven's sake?

STUDENT. Air Science.

STREPS.   And what's this?

STUDENT.   Geometry.

STREPS. What do they use that for?

STUDENT.   Surveying Land.

STREPS. You mean so we can annex it?

STUDENT. No, the whole earth.

STREPS.   That's excellent. You've got a good idea there. Treat 'em all alike.

STUDENT. [*showing a map*] And there's a map of the world. See,

206 **prison camp** the Greek refers specifically to Spartans captured at Pylos in 425 and kept in close confinement   223 **annex it** land taken from conquered enemies was divided among Athenian citizens

This is Athens.

    STREPS.   What are you talking about?

You're fooling; I can't see a single court in session.

    STUDENT. No, honestly. This here is Attica.

    STREPS. Then where's my hometown, and my friends
       and neighbors?   230

    STUDENT. There they are! And see here, where the
       coastline

Runs for miles? That's the island of Euboea.

    STREPS.   And who made it run?

Pericles and Athens! But where's Sparta?

    STUDENT.   Here.

    STREPS. Too close to Athens. Think of something, quick.

Move it away from us, a long way off.

    STUDENT. But that's impossible.

    STREPS.   That's just too bad

For you.

[SOCRATES *appears in midair. He is suspended in a basket,
              and looking at the sky.*]

       Hey, who's that fellow in the basket?

    STUDENT. Why, that's Himself.

    STREPS.   Himself?

    STUDENT.   That's Socrates.

    STREP: Hey, Socrates! [*to the* STUDENT] Give him a hail
       for me!

    STUDENT. Call him yourself, I'm busy   [*Exit.*]

    STREPS. Hey Soccy! Socrates!

    SOCRATES.   Are you addressing me,   240

You insect? What do you want?

    STREPS. Well, for a start you can tell me what you're
       doing.

    SOC. Walking on air and staring at the sun.

    STREPS. Well, if you must look down upon the gods

You have to go up in the air to do it.

    SOC. No doubt about it. I could never have

---

228 **court in session** Aristophanes frequently jokes about the
excessive litigiousness of the Athenians   232 **Euboea** long island
near coast of Attica which had revolted from Athens in 446
and was reconquered by Pericles   243 **Walking on air** a bur-
lesque of the meteorological interests of early philosophers. Socrates also, according to Plato, was keenly interested in astronomy

Discovered all these things above my head
Without suspending judgement, and developing
The natural sympathy between my subtle
250 Intellect and air. If I had kept my feet
On the ground, I could search up there for all eternity
And never find a thing! The earth exerts
An attraction on the essence of our thoughts:
The same applies to watercress.

    STREPS.   Come again?
Thought attracts the essence into watercress?
Come on, now, Socrates. Come down to my level
And teach me what I came to learn about.

    SOC. [*descending*] Why did you come?
    STREPS.   To learn to plead my case.
I'm bothered so with debts and creditors
260 I'm swamped, bled white, can't call my soul my own.

    SOC. How did you let yourself get in so deep?
    STREPS. I caught a horse-disease, a galloping consumption.
Come on, you have two sorts of argument.
Teach me the one that gets off without paying
And you can name your fee, so help me gods.

    SOC. So help you gods? The first thing you must learn
Is that the gods aren't legal tender here.

    STREPS. They're not? So what do you swear by? Wooden
    nickels?

    SOC. How would you like to learn the honest truth
About religion?
270   STREPS.   All considered, I'd be glad to.

    SOC. And hold communion with the Clouds, who are
Our deities?

    STREPS.   Just try and stop me.

    SOC. Then sit down on the sacred bed—
    STREPS.   [*doing so*]   I'm sitting.

    SOC. Now you must put this crown of sacred herbs
Upon your head—

    STREPS.   Herbs? Listen, Socrates,
It looks as if I'm being dressed up for the kill.

---

268 **Wooden nickels** literally "the iron money of Byzantium," a
state which still clung to coinage obsolete elsewhere   273 **sacred bed** perhaps a parody of some mystic rite

soc. Don't be nervous. This is what we always do
At initiations.
    STREPS.   What's in it for me?
    soc. You'll be a man who knows his way around,
A regular tongue twister of a fellow,   280
With spicy conversation.
    STREPS.   Spice is right, by god!
He's putting salt and pepper on me now!
    soc. Now let the old man hold his tongue, and pay
Decent attention. Let us pray.
[*adopting a liturgical tone*]   O mightiest
Of the mighty, boundless and immeasurable
Air, who hold our earth aloft so that it fall not,
Radiant Stratosphere, and worshipful divinities,
The Clouds, who thunder on us, yea, and lighten,
Arise and show yourselves in majesty to this
Your poor observer on the earth beneath.   290
    STREPS. Hey, hey, not so fast! Let me wrap up first.
I was an idiot, coming out without my hat.
    soc. Come then, O Clouds; in glory manifest
Yourselves, if now upon Olympus' crest
Snowbound you have your seat, or in the waters
Of Father Ocean go forth to the dance
So that the Nymphs behold and wonder; or
If with golden pitchers at the outflow of the Nile
You draw its waters, or hold court
By Lake Maiotis, or the snowy ridge of Mimas;   300
Accept the sacrifice we offer, and look down
With favor upon us who worship you.
    CHORUS OF CLOUDS. [*offstage*]

       Clouds that float free
       Let us rise so they may see us,
       Lightspun and dew, from the sounding
       Sea that is our father's, to the mane
       Green on the high hills; here
       Let us look eminent over the brimming
       Plain with its blessings, on the murmur
       And grace of water, on the deep voice   310

294 **Olympus** mountain home of the gods   300 **Maiotis** now the
Sea of Azov **Mimas** mountain on mainland of Asia Minor op-
posite island of Chios

Of the sounding sea; for heaven's eye
Is wide awake and bright, the sunlight
Shimmers, sparkles; brush away the dew
That wraps us, shows us goddesses,
And let us go wide-eyed into the world.

soc. O Clouds most illustrious, you have vouchsafed
My prayer an answer.
[*to* STREPSIADES]   Did you hear
The noise they made, that awful thunder roll?

STREPS. Great powers, I think you're marvellous. I'm so
upset

320 And scared out of my wits, I'm going to thunder
Right back in your faces. With your reverend permission
Or without it, I'm about to wet my pants.

soc. Cut out the horseplay and show respect.
The heavenly assembly is moved to sing.

CHORUS. [*offstage*]

So let us go
O sisters mine, rainbearers,
To the shining land, to Athena's
Domicile of heroes, the beloved
Soil of Cecrops, where is mystery

330 Of rites unspoken, where the portals of the shrine
Spread wide to believers. Gods
Go rich rewarded here, with images
And skyproud temples; here is praise of high
Processional, and sacrifice and feasting
Gay with garlands, as the year's face changes.
And at Spring's coming there is joy of Bacchus
With dancing and sweet voices matched in contest
And drone of pipers as the Muse gives tongue.

STREPS. For god's sake, Socrates, who are the ladies who
pronounced

340 So solemnly? Princesses out of fairytales?

soc. You couldn't be more wrong. They're clouds from
heaven,
The perfect deities for men who don't like work.

329 **Cecrops** mythical first king of Athens   336 **Bacchus** Dionysus, god of wine and drama   337 **matched in contest** the dramatic contests held in honor of Dionysus, such as the festival
at which the present play was performed

These are the ones who grant us insight, skill
In forensics, intelligence and paradox,
Doubletalk, spellbinding and humbuggery.
  STREPS. When I heard their voice my soul within me
     quivered,
And longs to split hairs, bicker over moonshine,
Pin down an argument and plead the negative.
So if possible I'd like to see them for myself.
  SOC. Looks towards Parnes. I can see them settling   350
Soft as a feather.
  STREPS.   Where? Show me!
  SOC.   They're coming
Thick now, filing over wood and valley—
  STREPS.   How come?
I can't see a thing.
  SOC. [*pointing offstage*] In the wings.
  STREPS.   Just a glimpse.

     [*The* CHORUS *files into the theater.*]

  SOC. You must see them now, if you're not stone blind.
  STREPS. God, yes! They're splendid, and they're every-
     where!
  SOC. And you had no idea that they were goddesses?
  STREPS. God, no! I always thought that they were mist
     and dew.
  SOC. Heaven forbid! They give protection to the soph-
     ists,
Quack doctors, gypsy fortune tellers, gigolos,
Popular songwriters, fake astrologers—   360
They'll offer their support to anyone who never
Held down an honest job, because they set their praise to
     music.
  STREPS. Then that's the reason they wrote "Stormy
     Weather,"
"On Top of Old Smoky," "Singing in the Rain,"
"Over the Rainbow," "Bye, Bye Blackbird,"
And "April Showers." By way of recompense
They dine off caviar and ortolans.
  SOC. They deserve to, don't they?
  STREPS. [*pointing to the* CHORUS] But what's happened
     to them?

350 **Parnes** mountain range in Attica due north of Athens

If they're really clouds, why do they look like women?
[*pointing to the sky*]
Those don't.

370   SOC.   And what do you think they look like?
STREPS. I'm not sure. Woolens hanging on the line.
Not in the least like women. [*pointing to the* CHORUS]
                              These have noses.
SOC. Let me ask you a question.
STREPS.   Hurry up, then, ask me.
SOC. Have you ever seen a cloud shaped like a centaur?
A leopard? Wolf? Bull?
STREPS.   Yes, of course. So what?
SOC. They take what shape they please. If they meet
        anyone
With a shaggy mop, like Xenophantes' boy,
They turn to centaurs, and make him look a fool.
STREPS. Suppose they meet Simon, who embezzled pub-
        lic funds?
380   SOC. They show him up by turning into wolves.
STREPS. They saw Cleonymus the coward yesterday;
He was trembling so much they turned into deer.
SOC. And now they're women; they must have just seen
        Cleisthenes!
STREPS. [*to the* CHORUS] Then welcome, noble ladies.
        Now if you have ever
Given tongue for anyone before, make heaven
Ring for me, your gracious majesties!
CHORUS. Welcome old man, ancient of days, who come
        hunting
Education; and you, high priest of perspicuous prolixity,
Say what you want; for of all transcendental
390 Philosophers, you are the only one—excepting Prodicus—
We care to listen to—him for his common sense
And understanding, you because you swagger through
        the streets

377 **Xenophantes' boy** Hieronymus, who had a mop of shaggy
hair   379 **Simon** details unknown: evidently a popular joke at
the time and used by other comic poets besides Aristophanes
381 **Cleonymus** one of Aristophanes' favorite butts, frequently
satirized for effeminacy and cowardice   383 **Cleisthenes** notorious homosexual   390 **Prodicus** sophist of high repute, particularly concerned with semantics

Squinting askance, barefooted, and because you have
So much to put up with, and are so very haughty
On the strength of our patronage.

STREPS. Mother earth!
What voice! How solemn, portentous and liturgical!

soc. Right! They alone are gods, the rest are hog-
wash.

STREPS. And that fellow on Olympus? Isn't Zeus a god?

soc. What Zeus? Stop driveling. There isn't any Zeus.

STREPS. No? Who sends rain, then? Answer that one
first.   400

soc. The Clouds, and I'll offer you substantial proof of
it.

Have you ever seen it raining when the Clouds weren't
there?
If Zeus sent rain, you would have thought the sky
Would be clear, and the Clouds be busy somewhere else.

STREPS. It figures, by Apollo. To this day
I've believed it was Zeus making water through a sieve.
But who makes thunder? That's what gives me the cold
shudders.

soc. The Clouds turning somersaults.

STREPS. Amazing!

soc. When they're saturated and set going by the law
of motion

They're held in equipoise, and as they're full of water   410
Collide by law of motion, and by virtue of their weight
Shatter each other and reverberate.

STREPS. But isn't it Zeus who passed this law of motion?

soc. No. It's a jar in the atmosphere.

STREPS. A jar? Well, well, you live
And learn. King Zeus is dead, long live King Jar!
But you've still said nothing of the rumble and the thun-
der.

soc. Weren't you listening? I said the humid clouds
Collide, and their density produces an explosion.

STREPS. Prove it!

---

414 **jar** in the atmosphere Anaxagoras, fifth century philosopher,
saw the origin of matter in a heavenly vortex which brought
elements into collision. Aristophanes puns on *dinos,* form of
dine, vortex, and *dinos,* goblet

SOC.   I'll use you as my working model.
It's a public holiday. You've stuffed yourself with meat
420   balls.
You have indigestion. What does your inside do? Rumble!
    STREPS. You're right, by Apollo! It plays up and churns
      around
And the meat balls boom like thunder, and the noise
Is dreadful; first, *piano,* burp. Then, *mezzoforte,*
Burp, burp. And when my bowels begin to open
It thunders BURP *fortissimo,* just like the clouds.
    SOC. Consider then: if from so small a belly
So great a blast can come, it's only reasonable
That air, which has no boundaries, can make loud thun-
    der.
430   That's why we use the same name in both cases—wind!
    STREPS. But where does fiery lightning come from, tell
      me that,
That carbonizes what it strikes, and singes what it misses?
It's Zeus, it must be, blasting unbelievers.
    SOC. You fool, you lunatic, you prehistoric fossil,
If it falls on men who take his name in vain
Why hasn't it hit Simon, Theorus or Cleonymus?
They do it all the time. But no, it hits his temples,
And Sunium, "the craggy top of Athens high,"
And great oaks. What have oak trees got to do with it?
440   The oak trees never take his name in vain.
    STREPS. Guess not. That's sense. But what is lightning
      then?
    SOC. When a sirocco, gaining altitude, is trapped
Inside the clouds, it inflates them like balloons.
The pressure builds, they burst (a law of physics),
It blows out and ignites itself through friction.
    STREPS. That's just what happened to me one spring
      picnic.
I was barbecuing a sausage for the family
And forgot to slit the skin. It swelled and swelled
And suddenly went bang. I smelt just like
450   An abattoir; my eyebrows both went up in flames.

436 **Simon** see v. 379 **Theorus** minor political figure and asso-
ciate of Cleon, for whom see v. 599n.   438 **Sunium** spectacular
promontory near Athens, site of temple of Poseidon

CHORUS. Mortal, who seek the store of wisdom that we
    have to offer,
Blest will you be in Athens and in Greece at large
If you are studious and mindful, and prepared to suffer
Hardship; if you falter not in standing or in going,
If you bear cold without shivering, or hunger without
    grievance,
Abstain from wine and exercise and other such frivolities,
And like a man of sense think this to be your greatest
    good:
Supremacy in rhetoric, deliberations and forensics.
    STREPS. Well, so far as an enduring spirit goes, and
    nagging
Speculation, and a griping stomach fed on turnip greens,   460
Don't worry about me. For what they're worth I'd gladly
Submit myself to any knocks you cared to give me.
    SOC. Then will you believe in no other god but these,
Our trinity: the Air in majesty, the Clouds, the Tongue?
    STREPS. I wouldn't give the rest so much as a good
    morning
If I met them in the street. I wouldn't sacrifice to them
Or pour them offerings, or burn incense on their altars.
    CHORUS. Take courage, then, and make your wishes
    known. We will not fail you
So long as you respect and honor us and cultivate intelli-
    gence.
    STREPS. Well, ladies, this is what I want—it isn't much: 470
To be far and away the best orator in Greece.
    CHORUS. Then your request is granted; and from this
    time on
No one will pass more motions in the House than you.
    STREPS. Don't talk to me of motions, I'm not so am-
    bitious.
I only want to twist the law and duck my creditors.
    CHORUS. Your dream will come true; it's a moderate
    request.
Take heart then, and entrust yourself to these our aco-
    lytes.
    STREPS. I put my trust in you and will obey—for I'm
    compelled to
By natural law, arising out of buying horses
And marrying a wife who ruined me.   480

I bequeath myself to these,
Let them treat me as they please,
Leave me hungry, thirsty too,
Freeze me, leave me black and blue,
Filthy me, on one condition:
Of my debts I have remission
And can win myself a name
As a stop-at-nothing, game
For any mischief, tongued with honey,
490　Minting lies as fast as money,
Full of bravado, never at a loss
For words, a scoundrel who can toss
Off stories at a second's notice,—if he chose
Could lie till he was purple, and who knows
The lawcourts inside out, a chatterbox,
A walking statute book, a cunning fox
Sharp as a pin, who'll tie you up in knots,
Deep as they come, who'll wriggle out of spots
Too tight for him, pull wool over your eyes,
500　A devil never in the same place twice,
A man who'll be the nuisance of your life, who'll
Snap up every unconsidered trifle. . . .

If I can win this name from our acquaintance
They can treat me any way they wish,
Even run my guts once through the mincer
And serve me to the students in a dish!
　　CHORUS. There's a dauntless spirit in him
Fittest for the fray. If you
Can master my instructions, your prestige
510　Will reach heights astronomical
Among man.
　　STREPS.　　And what's in it for me?
　　CHORUS. You'll share my lot, and be
For all the days remaining to you
The happiest man alive.
　　STREPS. Shall I ever live to see it?
　　CHORUS. Yes, there'll be crowds forever sitting
At your gates, desiring to consult with you
And ask your advice on actions and proceedings
Worth thousands, all of them crying out
For a talent like yours.
520　　　[*to* SOCRATES]　　But off you go

And begin the old man's education.
Stir up his mind, and take yourself
A sample of his intelligence.
    SOC. [*to* STREPSIADES] Come on, then. Give me an idea
    of what you're made of,
So I can know what battery of new
Techniques I must employ to break you down.
    STREPS. This isn't education, it's siege warfare!
    SOC. No, no, I just want to ask you a few questions.
How's your memory?
    STREPS.   It sort of varies.
If anybody owes me, excellent.   530
If I owe someone, blank. It's terrible!
    SOC. Do you have any natural gift for speaking?
    STREPS. Not speaking. But I've quite a gift for stealing.
    SOC. How can you learn, then?
    STREPS.   I'll make out, don't worry.
    SOC. Oh, very well. Now when I toss some scrap
Of scientific knowledge at you, see you catch it.
    STREPS. Are you going to feed me learning like dog
    biscuits?
    SOC. The man's an ignoramus, he's a savage!
I'm afraid you need some manners beaten into you.
By the way, what do you do if someone hits you?   540
    STREPS. I let him; count ten; take the names of wit-
    nesses;
Count ten again, then go call my attorney.
    SOC. All right! Take off your cloak.
    STREPS.   [*apprehensively*]   Have I been naughty?
    SOC. No, but it's customary to strip before you enter.
    STREPS. But I'm not hiding anything to plant on you!
    SOC. Come on, stop fooling. Off.
    STREPS. [*taking off his cloak*]   Then tell me this—
If I'm a good boy in school and pay attention
Which of the students shall I most take after?
    SOC. Chaerephon. There'll be no telling you apart.
    STREPS. Help! I'm going to turn into a spook!   550
    SOC. Stop playing the fool, and come along with me.
Come on, hurry up.

541 **names of witnesses** the target is again the litigiousness of
the Athenians

STREPS.   Well, give me a peace offering
To keep the ghosts away. I'm scared out of my wits!
It's just like visiting the catacombs!

[Exeunt into the Academy]

CHORUS. Then go your way in joy
　　Stouthearted; good luck go with him
　　Who though he has gone far along
　　Life's path, is bold to cast
　　The tint of novelty upon his days,
560　　And go pursuing wisdom.
[to the audience]
Ladies and gentlemen, I shall convey to you
　　The unimpeded truth, so help me Dionysus,
　　My only true begetter. As I hope to gain
　　First honors, and a reputation as a savant,
　　I took you for an audience of intelligence
　　And taste, and well deserving first sight of a comedy
　　Which was my cleverest yet, and cost me
　　No little sweat. But I was sent packing, while a gang
　　Of rednosed comics took the prizes that by rights
　　Were mine. And it was all your faults—yes, you, the
570　　critics;
　　It was on your account I went to so much trouble.
　　But some of you have sense, and I won't turn my back
　　　on you.
　　For ever since the day when my first offering
　　Was greeted with applause (the one about
　　The honest brother and the prodigal)
　　By men it was a pleasure to write plays for—
　　And I, still being immature to bring
　　Forth offspring, entrusted the production to another,

561 **Ladies and gentlemen** the *parabasis* (see Introduction pp. vi-viii) whose opening belongs to the revised version of the play and refers to the comedy's harsh reception by the original audience   569 **rednosed comics** Aristophanes' rivals Cratinus and Ameipsias   575 **The honest brother** Aristophanes' first comedy, *The Banqueters,* no longer extant, concerning a virtuous man who resided in the country and his brother corrupted by city vices   578 **entrusted . . . another** *The Banqueters* was produced by Callistratus; many of Aristophanes' comedies were staged by someone other than the author

And you then took it to your hearts, and gave it your
Support and your encouragement: yes, from that time
I've had proof of your critical intelligence.   580
So, like Electra in the tragedy,
Enter my comedy, to see if she can find
A public as enlightened as the first.
For if she sees the hair cut from her brother's head
She'll recognize it straightaway. Please mark the fact
That she's a decent self-respecting girl. To start with
There isn't any leather pink-tipped phallus
Dangling on her costume for the boys to laugh at,
No jokes about bald heads, no hoochy-coochy dances,
No old man covering the thinness of the dialogue   590
With slapstick; nor does she come on the scene
With blazing torches, screaming "Save me! Help!"
She comes with confidence—in herself and in her lines.
And though I'm such a poet I don't put on airs
Or try to fool you with the same old tricks
But always come with new material
For wit, no two alike and never dull.
When Cleon was on top I let him have it in the belly
But didn't have the heart to kick the man when he was
   down.
But my rivals! Once Hyperbolus has given them   600
A handhold, they're forever hitting him below the belt,

582 **Electra** in Aeschylus' *Libation Bearers* (458) Electra,
mourning by her father's grave, sees a lock of hair left by her
supposedly lost brother Orestes. She eventually identifies him
and there is a fond reconciliation. The same theme was treated
by Sophocles and Euripides.   588 **leather pink tipped phallus**
part of the traditional obscene costume of Old Comedy.
Throughout the *parabasis* Aristophanes is constantly asserting
that his comedy rises superior to such coarseness   590-593 **bald
heads . . . Help!"** more of the traditional comic business employed by Aristophanes' rivals. He uses most of these devices
himself while affecting to despise them   599 **Cleon** a demagogue prominent in Athens from 431 to his failure and death
ten years later, constantly feuding with Aristophanes because
of the attacks made on him in comedy, particularly in *The
Babylonians,* now lost, and *The Knights*   601 **Hyperbolus** another demagogue succeeding Cleon as the leader of the war
party, murdered by dissidents in 411

Yes, and his mother too. It was Eupolis began it
When he travestied my *Knights*, god damn his hide,
Then dragged his *Maricas* onto the stage
Sticking in this drunk old woman, just so she
Could dance the cancan—yes, the character
That Phrynichus invented years ago, the one
The sea serpent had for supper. Then Hermippus wrote
610   Another lampoon of Hyperbolus, and all
The others wrote their lampoons of Hyperbolus,
Stealing the image that I used, of men who fish
In troubled waters. Anyone who finds such things
Amusing needn't look for laughs in mine.
But if you take delight in me and my inventions
You'll win a lasting reputation for good taste.

     First summon I to sing with us
     Zeus, who is mightiest,
     Peerless among gods.
620   Then the most powerful
     Keeper of the trident
     Who restless makes earth
     And the salt waters tremble.
     Then the potent
     Name of our father
     Air, that gives all life,
     Holiest of the holy,
     And the driver of yoked horses

603 **his mother too** apparently a moneylender **Eupolis** fl. 430-410 and one of the greatest Old Comic writers. His **Maricas** attacked Hyperbolus as Aristophanes' **Knights** did Cleon; the two plays seem to have been sufficiently alike to prompt Aristophanes' charge of plagiarism here and Eupolis' retort that he had collaborated with Aristophanes 608 **Phrynichus** comic poet fl. 430-400, who in a parody of the tragic story of Andromeda had shown an old woman about to be eaten by a sea-monster 609 **Hermippus** comic poet whose *The Lady Breadsellers* (421-418) satirized Hyperbolus and his mother 612-613 **men who . . . waters** in *The Knights* vv. 864-7 Aristophanes compares the demagogues to fishers who muddy the water so they may trap eels more easily 621 **Keeper of the trident** Poseidon 628 **driver of yoked horses** the sun, conventionally represented as driving a burning chariot through the sky

Who fills the bowl of earth
With radiance and sunlight,   630
Divinity most powerful
Among gods and mortals.

All of you superintelligent people
In the audience, favor us with your attention.
We have a grievance, and we'll tell you to your faces.
We bring your city greater benefits
Than all the other gods, but we're the only ones
Who get no offerings or sacrifices from you—
And yet we're always watching out for you! If anyone
Is fool enough to go out when he shouldn't   640
We come with thunder or a shower of rain.
When you were voting for that godforsaken
Leatherbeater Cleon as your minister of war
We knit our brows and carried on like anything.
Then "cataracts and hurricanes spouted,"
The Moon eclipsed herself, the Sun lost not a minute
In turning down his wick, and swore he'd never
Shine on you again, if Cleon ever
Controlled the army. And you still elected him!
They say this state is naturally given   650
To folly, but however far you go astray,
The gods will make it turn out for the best.
And even this can be a blessing in disguise!
This we can demonstrate with ease. If you convict
Cleon, that cormorant, of bribery and peculation,
And shut his trap, and clap him in the pillory,
It'll be the same old story; even
Your mistakes will bring you credit in the end!

Apollo, O my lord
Of Delos, dweller on   660
The crested peak of Cynthus,
Once more invest me.
And you who are housed

633-658 **All of you . . . in the end** written for the first production of the play; note that Cleon, referred to as finished in v. 600
is represented as still thriving here   660 **Delos** traditional island
birthplace of Apollo, of which **Cynthus** is the highest mountain

Golden in Ephesus, the blessed one
To whom girls of Lydia
Pay orisons, and you
Who dwell among us, ours,
Athena, who with brandished ægis
Guard our citadel;
670   And the bright one, dweller
On the mountain Parnassus
As the torchlight marks you
In the rout of wild women,
The reveler Dionysus.

When we were ready for our journey here
The Moon stopped by with a message for you:
"First, to Athens and the friends of Athens, greeting."
Then, that she was cross with you, she'd been hard done
      by,
After she'd always done her best to help you
680   And not just talked about it—first, by saving you
A bit each month on light bills, so much in fact
That anyone going out to spend the evening
Would say "Don't light that torch, the moon shines
      bright."
She claims she's benefited you in other ways,
But you make nonsense of the calendar
And turn it haywire, so the gods, she says,
Hold her to blame whenever they are cheated
Out of their supper, and must come back home
Without the feast the calendar had promised them.
690   And that's not all of it. When you should be in church
You're in the lawcourts putting screws on people.
And when the gods observe a fast in memory
Of the war-dead (Trojan War, of course)

---

664 **Ephesus** rich city of **Lydia** in Asia Minor, centre of the cult
of Artemis, Apollo's sister, the goddess referred to here   668
aegis the magic mantle of Athena, her wonderworking goatskin
671 **Parnassus** mountain near Delphi, haunt of Apollo and
Dionysus   685 **calendar** important calendar reforms by the
astronomer Meton in 432, designed to correlate the lunar
month and the solar year, were apparently still causing confusion

You're drinking, having fun. It was to pay you back
   for this
That when Hyperbolus this year was made Recorder
We goddesses deprived him of his crown of office.
Perhaps he'll find it easier to remember in the future
That you must organize your life by the Moon's phases.

[*Enter* SOCRATES *angrily from the Academy.*]

SOC. So help me Air and Space and Respiration,
I never saw a more cantankerous   700
Illiterate old knucklehead. No sooner
Does he take a spark or two of wit
Into his head, than out they pop again,
Before they've entered! But I'll call him out
Into the sun. Yoohoo, Strepsiades!
Come on outdoors, and bring your bedroll with you!

[*Enter* STREPSIADES *from the Academy, struggling with
his bed.*]

STREPS. The bugs won't let me get away with it.
SOC. Give over. Drop it. Pay attention. [STREPSIADES
   does so]
                           There.
Now tell me where you'd like to start your lessons.
Where shall we start from scratch? You name it.   710
What shall it be? Scales, harmony or grammar?
STREPS. Let's do some scales. The other day a seedsman
Cheated me of three pints with his scales.
SOC. I don't mean that! I'm talking about music!
Which do you like best, thirds or fourths?
STREPS. There's nothing I like better than a fifth myself.
SOC. That's utter nonsense.
STREPS.   What will you bet me now
That five fifths make four quarts?
SOC. Oh, go to hell, you clod, you nincompoop.
Perhaps you'll find that harmony comes easier.   720
STREPS. What's harmony got to do with liquid measure?
SOC. First it will teach you how to be a man

695 **Hyperbolus** see v. 601. Details unknown; apparently his
official wreath had blown off during a public ceremony

Of culture in society, and tell the difference
Between *alla marcia* and *pizzicato*.

STREPS. What's *pizzicato*?

SOC.   Playing with your fingers.

STREPS. Playing with your fingers? Why, that's nothing!
When I was a kid I could play with my toes!

SOC. You stupid clown!

STREPS.   Now don't upset yourself.
That isn't what I came to learn.

SOC.   What was it, then?

STREPS. One thing and one thing only—unfair argu-
730   ment.

SOC. But there are certain course prerequisites;
For instance, knowing the names of the male quadrupeds.

STREPS. If I didn't I should have my head examined.
The males are ram, goat, bull, dog, cock.

SOC. That's very good. Now list the feminines.

STEPS. The feminines? Sheep, nanny, moocow, bitch
and cock.

SOC. You see what happened? You're using the same
names
For masculine and feminine alike.

STREPS. How do you mean? Do tell.

SOC.   Well, cock and cock.

STREPS. Ye gods and little fishes! Well, what should I
740   say?

SOC. If the male's a cock, the female's a coquette.

STREPS. A coquette? By the Air, that's marvellous!
That lesson alone's worth something, so I'll tell you what:
Give me your breadpan and I'll fill him up for you.

SOC. More ignorance! You called the breadpan "him."
Now everybody knows a breadpan is a vessel,
A vessel is a ship, and ships are feminine.

STREPS. I made it masculine?

SOC.   Of course you did.
Just like Cleonymus.

724 **pizzicato** the Greek text has been adapted here to make the
joke meaningful in English. The original puns on the two mean-
ings of *daktylos,* dactylic metre and finger   745 **You called
. . . him** the Greek joke arises from the difference between
masculine and feminine in the definite article and noun termination, and cannot be reproduced in English as it stands

STREPS.   Cleonymus? I'm not with you.

SOC. Cleonymus has a masculine termination.   750

STREPS. Oh no he hasn't, not Cleonymus!

Well, what am I to call it after this?

SOC. The masculine is "pan," the feminine is "pansy."

STREPS. The feminine is "pansy?"

SOC.   That's the way.

STREPS. I see! A pansy, like Cleonymus!

SOC. You still have to master proper names

And know the masculines and feminines.

STREPS. I know which ones are feminines.

SOC.   Recite.

STREPS. Lysilla, Philinna, Cleitagora, Demetria.

SOC. Tell me some men's names.

STREPS.   I know millions.   760

Philoxenos, Melesias, Amynias—

SOC. You idiot, those names aren't masculines!

STREPS. Not masculines?

SOC.   No, nothing of the sort.

Amynias, now. Is that a surname?

STREPS.   No.

SOC. Exactly! If it's not a sir name

It must be a lady's name!

STREPS.   And doesn't he

Deserve it? He was never in the service.

Why tell me things that everybody knows?

SOC. It doesn't matter. Into bed.

STREPS.   What for?   770

SOC. Another autotherapeutic session.

STREPS. No, no, not in that bed again! No, if I have

To think, then let me do it lying on the ground!

SOC. Go on. No argument.

STREPS. [lying down]   Good grief,

The bugs will have their pick of me today!

SOC. Now put on your thinking cap

And scrutinize and contemplate.

Look at things from every angle.

If you're caught in a dilemma

749 **Cleonymus** see v. 381. His ambiguous gender makes him an apt object for comparison 764 **Amynias** the Greek joke arises from the fact the vocative of the masculine Amynias, Amynia, resembles a feminine nominative

780 Drop it, shift your point of view.
Honied sleep must stand at bay. [*Exit*.]
    STREPS. Ooch! Ouch!
    CHORUS. What's the matter? Did it hurt?
    STREPS. Help, it's agony, I'm dying!
All the bugs are creeping out
From the bedding, biting me,
Having dinner off my ribs,
Drinking up my breath of life,
Sinking teeth into my manhood,
790 Excavating in my bottom,
Oh, oh, oh, they're killing me!
    CHORUS. Don't make so much fuss about it.
    STREPS. Make no fuss? I've lost my money,
Lost my lifeblood, my complexion,
Lost my slipper; in addition
As I hummed myself a ditty
To amuse me on my vigil
I was almost gone myself.

[*Reenter* SOCRATES.]

    SOC. Hey, what's this? You're not thinking!
    STREPS.   Me?
Of course I am.
800   SOC.   And what about?
    STREPS. Whether the bugs will leave a bit of me.
    SOC. Drop dead.
    STREPS.   My friend, that's exactly what I'm doing.
    SOC. No weakening. Pull up the clothes again.
You have to think of some smart stratagem
To cheat your creditors.
    STREPS. [*pulling the blankets over his head*] I only wish
That I could pull the wool over their eyes
As easily as I can pull this over mine.

[*A brief pause, while* STREPSIADES *cogitates*.]

    SOC. Right! What's he doing? Peekaboo!
Have you gone back to sleep?
    STREPS.   No I have not.
    SOC. Got something?
    STREPS.   God, no.
810   SOC.   Not a single thing?

STREPS. Well, you could say I'm taking myself in hand.

SOC. Pull up the clothes again and think.

STREPS. Think about what? You tell me, Socrates.

SOC. I'll tell you, if you tell me what you want.

STREPS. You know! I've told you a million times already!
My debts! I don't want to have to pay them.

SOC. Come, come, wrap up. You must be sensitive and
subtle.

Examine every aspect of the case minutely
And analyse your problem.

STREPS.   Oh, good grief!

SOC. Don't interrupt. And if you find yourself in trouble, 820
Leave it for a moment; then return,
Pick up the thought again and weigh it well.

STREPS. Hey, Soc!

SOC.   All right, old boy, what is it now?

STREPS. I have an idea how to cut my losses.

SOC. Let's have it.

STREPS.   Tell me what you think of this—

SOC. What?

STREPS.   Just suppose I hire a witch from Thessaly
One night to conjure down the moon, and then
Shut it up tight inside a hatbox
And keep it there, like a looking glass.

SOC. And what good would that do you?

STREPS.   What good would— 830
Why, if the moon should never rise again
I'd never have another payment due.

SOC. Why?

STREPS.   Interest is reckoned by the month!

SOC. Bravo! Now I'll toss you another problem.
You're taken to court; they fine you a small fortune.
Tell me how you'd get out of that one.

STREPS. I'd . . . I'd . . . I'd have to think it over.

SOC. Don't obfuscate yourself in introspection.
Let your thoughts wander, give them scope,
Like beetles with a thread tied round their legs. 840

STREPS. Got it! A way out! This is surely ingenious.
Come on, admit it.

SOC.   Well, tell me what it is.

826 **Thessaly** in the north of Greece, traditional abode of
witches

STREPS. Haven't you seen in the druggists' shops
That beautiful transparent stone
They use for lighting fires?
    SOC.   A burning glass?
    STREPS. That's what I mean. I'd get my hands on one
And as the clerk was writing down the charges
I'd stand at a distance on the sunny side
And burn up the letters. How about that?
    SOC. Ingenious, by the Graces.
850   STREPS.   Gee, it's wonderful
To wipe out an enormous fine like that.
    SOC. Get your teeth into this one.
    STREPS.   What is it now?
    SOC. How would you stop a suit against you
When there was nobody to testify on your side
And you were bound to lose?
    STREPS.   Couldn't be simpler.
    SOC. Right, what's the answer?
    STREPS.   Here it is:
When there was one case still to go
Before they got to mine, I'd hang myself.
    SOC. Don't be ridiculous.
    STREPS.   I'm not, by god.
860 They couldn't prosecute me after I was dead.
    SOC. Get out, you fool. I'll give you no more lessons.
    STREPS. Why not? Oh please do, Socrates.
    SOC. As soon as I teach you something you forget it.
What was the first thing that you learned? Come on!
    STREPS. The first thing I learned? The first thing . . .
    now what was it?
What do you call that thing we keep the bread on?
Oh, what was it?
    SOC.   You can go to hell.
You silly old coot, you've a mind like a sieve.

[*Exit* SOCRATES *into the Academy.*]

    STREPS. Oh, dear, whatever will become of me?
870 This is the end; I haven't learned to speak.
Clouds, give me some advice. What can I do?
    CHORUS. This is our advice, old man, to you:
If you have a son and heir at home
Enroll him as a pupil in your place.

STREPS. I have a son all right—a gentleman,
But college bores him. What am I to do?
    CHORUS. You let him give the orders?
    STREPS.   Well, he's young and active.
And inherited his mother's airs and graces.
But I'll go hunt him out, and if he still won't come
I'll throw him out, and no one's going to stop me. [*Exit.*]   880
    CHORUS. [*turning to the house and addressing* SOCRATES]
        Don't you see how we alone
        Of gods can shower our blessings on you?
        He is now prepared to do
        Whatever you command him to.
But now you've hypnotized him and got him on a string
Don't lose a second, get your hands on every little thing
You can; for in cases like these
The picture can change with ease.

[ENTER STREPSIADES, *driving* PHEIDIPPIDES *out of the
                    house.*]

    STREPS. So help me Fog in heaven, you're not staying
        here!
Get out! Get fat on Megacles's masonry!   890
    PHEID. Father, what in the world's got into you?
Olympian Zeus, have you lost your mind?
    STREPS. Olympian Zeus! How stupid can you get,
Believing in Zeus, at your age!
    PHEID. What's so funny?
    STREPS.   It's preposterous,
A kid like you believing such old-fashioned stuff.
Come over here, I'll tell you a thing or two:
Get this in your head, and you'll really be grown up.
But don't you breathe it to a single living soul!
    PHEID. All right, what is it?
    STREPS.   You just swore by Zeus.   900
    PHEID. I did.
    STREPS.   Now observe the blessings of education.
Pheidippides, there isn't any Zeus.
    PHEID.   Who is there, then?
    STREPS. Jar is the king now. He kicked Zeus out.
    PHEID. Why, that's ridiculous!
    STREPS.   It's the honest truth.
    PHEID. Who says so?

STREPS.   Socrates the Melian,
And Chaerephon, the great fleafootprintologist.
   PHEID. Have you completely lost your mind?
Listening to these lunatics?
   STREPS.   Wash out your mouth!
Don't let me hear you say another word
910 Against them. They know what they're doing, they've
Got what it takes. You don't see them waste money
On barbers, haircream and deodorants,
Or visiting the bath house to get clean.
I might as well be dead, the way you've cleaned me out!
Don't waste another moment. Help me. Go take lessons.
   PHEID. What do they have to teach you that's worth
       knowing?
   STREPS. Are you serious? The sum of human wisdom.
You'll know yourself, how thick and dense you are.
But wait a moment, I'll be back directly. [*Exit.*]
920 PHEID. What shall I do? My father's gone insane.
I don't know whether to have him committed
Or warn the undertakers he's delirious.

       [*Reenter* STREPSIADES *with two fowls.*]

   STREPS. Now take a look at this. What would you call it?
   PHEID. A cock.
   STREPS.   Very good. What about this one?
   PHEID. A cock.
   STREPS.   Both of them? You've made a howler.
Don't ever say that again. Call the male bird
A cock, and the female a coquette.
   PHEID. Coquette, eh? So that's the sort of thing
This mine of wisdom's taught you. Very clever.
930   STREPS. Oh, that's not all. But it all goes in one ear
And out the other, I'm so old and stupid.
   PHEID. And so it was for this you lost your cloak!
   STREPS. I didn't lose it, I was absent-minded.
   PHEID. And what have you done with your shoes, you
       old fool?

905 **Melian** from the island of Melos. Socrates was Athenian,
and there may be confusion here, deliberate or otherwise, with
the sceptical philosopher Diagoras, a native of the island   932
cloak taken from him by Socrates, v. 543. See also v. 1593

STREPS. As Pericles would say, they went into the
  general fund.
Come on, stir yourself, let's go. Do your father this one
  favor
Then you can sow your wild oats as you please.
I remember when you were only six years old
I took you to the fair, and you looked up at me
And said "Buy 'ickle me a wagon," and I spent   940
Half of my first day's jury-wages on you.
  PHEID. All right, I'll go. But some day you'll be sorry.
  STREPS. Good boy for doing what your father says.

  [*They walk across to* SOCRATES' *Academy.*]

                                            Hey, Socrates!
Come out; I'm bringing you this boy of mine.
It took a lot of arguing.

              [*Enter* SOCRATES.]

  SOC.   Poor little fellow,
A freshman; ignorant of Hanging Basketry!
  PHEID. You're pretty fresh yourself. I hope they soon
    hang you.
  STREPS. Damnation! Don't be rude to the professor!
  SOC. [*imitating* PHEIDIPPIDES' *accent*] "Thoon hang
    you!" What kind of accent's that?
Slipshod diction! How can he ever master   950
Mitigating circumstances, Cross-examination
And the art of Forensical Obscurity?
Hyperbolus passed, though—for a high fee, naturally.
  STREPS. Don't worry, give him lessons. He was born
    sharpwitted.
When he was only a little boy so high
He'd sit indoors and build his blocks, carve boats,
Make wagons out of old shoes, toy frogs
Out of pomegranates, you never would believe it.
So teach him both the arguments you have—
The Better one, whichever that is, and the Worse,

935 **As Pericles would say** the statesman had used public money
to buy off certain enemies of Athens, and was naturally re-
luctant to explain where it had gone. When pressed for an
explanation he answered only in the vaguest terms

The one the man who doesn't have an honest case
Can use to overturn the Better. If you can
960 Only teach him one of them, then teach the Worse.
    SOC. All right. He'll hear them arguing in person.
I won't be here.
    STREPS.   But don't forget to give him
Answers for any lawful accusations.

[*Exeunt* SOCRATES *and* STREPSIADES. *Enter* TRUE LOGIC *and*
    FALSE LOGIC. *They are dressed as fighting cocks.*]

    TRUE LOGIC. Come on out and show yourself
To the folks, you blowhard!
    FALSE LOGIC. Lead on, True Logic! It'll please me all the
    more
970 If there's a crowd to see me smash you.
    T.L. Smash me? Who do you think you are?
    F.L. Logic.
    T.L.   Yes, the inferior sort.
    F.L. But I'll beat you, although they tip
You as the favorite.
    T.L.   What makes you so smart?
    F.L. Me? I'm an original!
    T.L.   Yes, it's all the idiots around
Who keep you in business.
    F.L.   No, it's the wise men.
    T.L. I'll tear you apart!
    F.L.   How?
Do tell!
    T.L. By telling the truth.
    F.L. I'll fix you! I'll match that one.
980 I say there's no such thing as Truth or Justice.
    T.L. You say there's. . . .
    F.L.   Well, where is it, then?
    T.L. In heaven, where the gods are.
    F.L. And if there's any justice, how
Could Zeus truss up his father and
Not die for it?
    T.L.   The man's a running
Sewer; hey, fetch me a basin, quick.

984 **Zeus . . . father** in the traditional theogony Zeus, son of
Cronus, attacked his father and became chief god himself

F.L. Get wise. You're obsolete.

T.L. Why, you unnatural . . . where's your decency?

F.L. Thanks for the bouquet.

T.L.   You parasite!

F.L. Such flowery compliments!

T.L.   You'd murder your own father! 990

F.L. You're gilding me with praises if you only knew it.

T.L. Gold are they now? The old days thought them
lead.

F.L. And now it's an unparalleled distinction.

T.L. Don't push your luck.

F.L.   Museum piece!

T.L. And it's on account of you
That the kids stay home from school!
But Athens will wake up one day
And see the sort of things you teach, the fools!

F.L. You lousy beggar.

T.L.   You and your smart clothes.   1000
But you were in the gutter once yourself,
Telling everybody you were Telephus
And chewing on a lunchbag full of nothing.

F.L. Many a true word spoken in jest!

T.L. Many the fools who keep you alive
To destroy their young with your insanity!

F.L. [gesturing towards PHEIDIPPIDES]
He'll learn nothing from you—you're as old as the hills.

T.L. Then he must be rescued straight away—
You'll teach him nothing but silly chatter.

F.L. [to PHEIDIPPIDES] Come over here, and leave him
to his gibberish.

T.L. Hands off him, or I'll make you howl for it!   1010

CHORUS. [to TRUE LOGIC]
Stop your fights and abuse
And give demonstration
Of the lessons you taught
To the past generation.
                    [to FALSE LOGIC]
And you, give account
Of the New Education,

1001 **Telephus** beggarly prince in Euripides' notorious tragedy,
438

So he can hear both
And choose *his* destination.
　　T.L. Well, I'm agreeable.
　　F.L.　　　　　　　　　　That goes for me too.
1020　CHORUS. All right, who'll open the debate?
　　F.L. I'll yield the privilege to him,
And out of his own mouth I'll take
The thoughts, the sentiments and syllogisms
To put him down. And in the last resort
If he so much as opens up his mouth
To clear his throat, I'll hit him smack between the eyes
With some penetrating, devastating apothegm.
　　CHORUS. All right! Speak with confidence, both of you:
Be sensible, subtle and smart.
1030　See which is the better debater.
They're off! And my friends here await a
High test of forensical art.
　　　　　　　　　　[*to* TRUE LOGIC]
Now you, who gave the older generation
The glory of so many blameless characters
Speak as you feel inclined, and tell us all
About yourself!
　　T.L. My subject is the schooling that our state enjoyed
　　　　before,
When I told the truth and flourished, and when decency
　　　　was law.
First, "Children should be seen and never heard"—that
　　　　was the rule,
And in orderly procession they would march to music
1040　　　school
With their neighbors, stripped for action though the snow·
　　　　was falling bleak,
And they learned to sing good music, not to cuddle cheek
　　　　to cheek,
Like "Praise the god of battles" and "The far-off sound of
　　　　war,"
To the good old-fashioned melodies their fathers sang
　　　　before.
And if anybody tried to jazz it up and play the fool
With the syncopated harmonies of Phrynis and his school
1046 **Phrynis** fl. 450, a composer who added several embellish-
ments to the traditionally rigid musical patterns

He'd be beaten for his trouble as a proven music-hater.
Then they'd sit up straight and decent, so the casual spec-
tator
Wouldn't have his eye offended by indelicate exposure,
And they'd take good care to smooth the sand beneath
them, at the closure   1050
Of their classes, so they wouldn't leave temptation for
admirers.
They used no oils or unguents, nor was any lad desirous
Of developing a bloom of down, at least below the waist.
They never cooed or simpered, or their manly sex dis-
graced,
Mincing through the streets like harlots, giving out the old
come-hither;
And spicy foods, like radishes, they'd pass up altogether.
They'd let their elders help themselves to relish and
hors d'oeuvres;
Gulping, laughing, playing footsy—why, they'd never
have the nerve!
    F.L. This stinks of harvest festivals, and hymns, and hair
in buns,
And weekly go-to-meetings.
    T.L.   Yes, but these rules are the ones 1060
That produced a race of heroes and the battles that we
won!
But you teach boys to muffle up the minute that they're
born;
I nearly choke with anger when I'm at the city sports
And see the boys with shield held close because they're
cold in shorts.
[*to* PHEIDIPPIDES] So there, my boy! You vote for me—my
argument's the stronger,
And you won't haunt street corners or the bathhouse any
longer.
You'll learn to hate immodesty, for scorn have little care,
To rise when elders enter and to offer them your chair,
To wear the badge of Modesty upon your heart, and shun
Wrongdoing, be a dutiful and everloving son,   1070
To flee the door of chorus-girls and others of that station
For fear they'll send you valentines and ruin your repu-
tation,
Nor to answer back your father or to call him out-of-date

Or repay him for his childhood care with callousness and
    hate.

    F.L. [*gesturing towards* TRUE LOGIC]

If you listen to what *he* says, then a kinship you'll enjoy
With the litter of Hippocrates, they'll call you "mommy's
    boy."

    T.L. You'll spend your time at exercise, your skin will
    bloom and shine,

Not argue trivialities, not bicker, snarl or whine
In court or on street corners like the youths that now we
    see,

1080 But go down to the sports field, and beneath the olive tree
Run races crowned with rushes, with an understanding
    friend
Of your own age and persuasion, and whose tastes and
    morals tend
To a temperate discretion, in a place of rest and peace
Where honeysuckle scents the air, and leaves of linden
    trees
Make a carpet for your running, where the breezes
    sigh and sing
From the plane-tree to the elm-tree in the splendor of the
    spring.

      If you do as I say
      And go my way
      Your skin will glow,
1090   Your biceps grow,
      Your tongue will shrink,
      You're in the pink!
      You'll grow plump at the rear,
      Less protuberant here.
      But, oh, if you follow the youth of today
      Your shoulders will slump, your complexion turn gray,
      Oversexed and undercut,
      Long in tongue and short in butt,
      Ever prone to pass a motion,
1100   For he'll feed you with the notion
      Fair is foul and foul is fair.
      Also if you don't take care

1076 **Hippocrates** probably Pericles' nephew and Athenian
general

Tar you with the filthy brush
Of that swine Antimachus.

CHORUS. O you who set up wisdom
On a pedestal of glory
What delectable discretion
Is apparent in your story!
Heaven bless the good old days.
                    [*to* FALSE LOGIC]
Now, destroyer of tradition,   1110
Utter something sharp and novel,
For you have stiff competition.
    F.L. My guts are on fire, I had such a desire
To answer his charges and wave them away.
I'm known as "the Worse' to the schools—I was first
A denial of justice and law to display.
And that's worth a million in silver—a trillion!
To choose the wrong argument, then win the case.
I'll smash by citation his prized education.
He starts by proclaiming hot baths a disgrace.   1120
                    [*to* TRUE LOGIC]
Come now: you abhor such delights. With what cause?
    T.L. They make men decrepit and unfit for use.
    F.L. Hold on! For I've got you at once where I want
    you.
Now tell me: which one of the children of Zeus
Was most valiant, loyal and performed the most toil?
    T.L. I'd name Heracles, most courageous of men.
    F.L. Have you seen Heracles' Cold Baths, if you please?
But who's braver than he?
    T.L.   See, he's at it again!
The same cock-and-bull that makes bath-houses full
Of the young of the city, who should be in training. 1130
    F.L. You dislike public meeting? It's good, I repeat:
If it were bad, we'd see Homer refraining

1104 **Antimachus** Athenian notorious for immorality 1126
Heracles the demi-god, son of Zeus and the mortal Alcmena
1127 **Heracles' Cold Baths** custom associated Heracles' name
with *warm* springs. According to legend the first such spring
had appeared from the ground to refresh the hero when he was
exhausted after one of his labors.

From making old Nestor hold forth, and the rest
Of the wise. Now, he claims exercise
Isn't good for the tongue when it's done by the young,
And that boys should be chaste. On both I demur.
Has chastity ever brought benefits? Never!
If you know any, give me your answer, good sir.

  T.L. Yes, many! Take one—the sword Peleus won.

1140 F.L. Sword! That was a wonderful present, poor devil.
Hyperbolus holds a small fortune in gold,
By Zeus, not a sword, through his fondness for evil.

  T.L. And Peleus, modest, wed Thetis, a goddess.

  F.L. And then she deserted him, found him too dull.
He acted like dead when he flopped into bed:
Women like to be roughly manhandled, old fool.

      [*to* PHEIDIPPIDES]

Now listen, my son, and consider the fun
That you'll lose if you lead a chaste, modest existence:
No women, no boys, no drinking, no joys
Of the banquet—what's life worth without such assist-
1150 ance?
All right! I'll turn next to the lusts of the flesh.
You've been naughty, made love to another man's wife.
You're jailed without plea. If you take up with me
You can rut, you can roar, have the time of your life.
If you're caught in the act you can answer in fact
That you're innocent. Quote the example of Zeus.
He was never above pretty women and love,
And if the gods do it, men have an excuse!

  T.L. But what if they catch him, castrate him and
    scratch him
1160 And make him a fairy through listening to you?

    F.L. A fairy? So what? There are worse things, a lot!

    T.L. There are worse? Well, supposing you name one or
    two.

1133 **Nestor** oldest and wisest of the Greeks in Homer's *Iliad*,
who advises the younger warriors during the Trojan War
1139 **Peleus** mythical hero of several adventures; he refused
Astydameia, wife of King Acastus, when she attempted to se-
duce him. She thereupon falsely accused him and her husband
plotted his death, but he was saved by a god-given sword
1143 **Thetis** sea-deity given to Peleus as a reward for his virtue; their son was Achilles, mightiest Greek warrior at Troy
1156 **Zeus** had many love affairs with mortal women

T.L. What will you say if I win this argument?

F.L. Not another word.

T.L.   All right then, here we go:
Who make up the courts of law?

T.L. Fairies!

F.L.   Very true, I'm sure.
And the playwrights and the poets?

T.L. Fairies all of them!

F.L.   I know it!
Politicians? What of them?

T.L. Fairies all!

F.L.   You're right again!   1170
Now you see your big mistake.
If you want examples, take
The audience.

T.L.   I'm looking now.

F.L. What do you see there?

T.L.   Row on row
Of fairies! Heaven help me! Wow!
That man's one of them—and how!
And that one, sitting over there,
The fellow with the knee-length hair.

F.L. What do you say?

T.L.   Here, take my cloak:
I yield to you, you fairy folk.   1180
I'll no more argue by contraries:
Move over! I believe in fairies!

[*Exeunt* TRUE *and* FALSE LOGIC. *Enter* SOCRATES
and STREPSIADES.]

SOC. What shall it be? Do you want to take your son
Away, or shall I teach him how to speak?

STREPS. Teach him, don't spare the rod, and just remem-
        ber,
Sharpen his wit on both sides, one
For small offenses, and the other cutting edge
For matters of more consequence.

SOC.   Don't worry.
He'll be a splendid sophist when we've done with him.

STREPS. Poor devil, with no color in his cheeks.   1190

[*Exeunt* SOCRATES *and* PHEIDIPPIDES *to the Academy,*
STREPSIADES *to his house.*]

CHORUS. Then go. But I've a feeling you'll be sorry.
And now we're anxious to inform our judges
What they'll win if they treat our chorus right.
First, when the season comes to turn the soil
We'll rain on you first, and keep the others waiting.
What's more, we'll oversee your crops and vineyards
And keep off press of drought, and cloudbursts too.
But if any mortal slights us who are goddesses
Let him watch out! We'll give him lots of trouble.
1200 He'll get no wine, no anything from his acreage.
As soon as buds show on the vine and olive
They'll be knocked off when we do our target practice.
And if we see him laying bricks we'll come
With rain and hail to whip his tiles from over him.
If he, a friend or a relation's getting married
We'll rain all night, so that he'd probably
Prefer the drought of Egypt to voting wrong today.

[*Enter* STREPSIADES *from his house.*]

STREPS. Five, four, three, and after three comes two,
And then the day of all days that I loathe,
1210 Detest, abominate—the day that follows,
The last day of the old moon and the first day of the new.
And every single person I owe money to
Has sworn he'll risk the costs and start an action
To ruin me and utterly destroy me.
And when I ask a modest favor, nothing more
Than I'm entitled to—"Now listen, friend,
Forgive me part of it, and give me extra time

1193 **treat our chorus right** a frank appeal for votes in the dramatic contest   1211 **The last day . . . of the new** in the old
Greek lunar calendar months were alternately 30 and 29 days
each; the moon's orbit of 29½ days meant that the new moon
always fell on the last day of the month. At the beginning of
the day the moon was waning, at the end waxing: hence the
"last day of the old moon and the first day of the new" is one
and the same day. Pheidippides, to confuse Strepsiades' creditors, wilfully confuses moon and month, and insists on regarding
it as a two-day period   1213 **risk the costs** in Athenian legal
practice the plantiff was required to deposit a sum varying according to the amount involved with the court before bringing
suit. The translation slightly adapts the idea to employ more
familiar modern legal terminology

To pay the rest"—they say they wouldn't touch it
On those terms, shout abuse at me and say
I've swindled them, they'll have the law on me.   1220
So let them go ahead and see if I care,
Providing Pheidippides has learnt to speak.
Well, there's a quick way of finding out.
Here's the Academy. I'll knock on the door.
Hey, anybody home? [knocking]

[Enter SOCRATES from the ACADEMY.]

SOC.   Strepsiades!
How good to see you!
     STREPS.   Likewise. Here, before
You say another word, grab hold of this. [giving a present]
You have to give an apple to the teacher.
And tell me if my son has learnt the argument
That you brought out for us a while ago.   1230
     SOC. He's learnt it.
     STREPS.   Praised be Saint Rascality!
     SOC. Now you can get out of any suit you please.
     STREPS. Suppose there are witnesses to swear I borrowed
          money?
     SOC. Let 'em all come! The more the merrier!
     STREPS. Then shall my song sound loud and deep:
Weep, weep, you pennypinchers, weep!
Farewell the principal and compound interest,
Nothing shall harm me more.
Oho, oh joy! Oh what a boy
Is being raised beneath this roof   1240
To stand up for me, the protector
Of his father's house, the downfall of my enemies,
His father's savior in his hour of need!
Run and call him out to me;
Come forth, my son, come forth, my child,
Your father speaks!

[Enter PHEIDIPPIDES.]

     SOC. And here he is.
     STREPS. My jewel, my joy!

1235-1251 Then shall my song . . . come here to pa a sus-
tained passage of tragic parody, probably performed with appropriate delivery and gestures

soc. Here, take the boy!

1250 STREPS. Oho, aha,
Come here to pa!
It's wonderful to see you! What a color!
Look at you! There's contradiction written
All over your face, argumentation
And good old native cussedness—"What's that you say?"—
Sprouting like crazy. You've a proper look about you
Of criminals who hit a man and holler
"He hit me first!" Yes, you look like
A regular old son of Attic soil.

1260 All right. Now get me out of this disaster.
You got me into it.

PHEID. What's biting you?

STREPS. The old-and-new moon day.

PHEID. You're telling me that there's an old-and-new
moon day?

STREPS. Yes, that's the deadline, when they tell me that
They're going to stake their money in the courts.

PHEID. They'll lose it if they do. Whatever made you
Think that one day could be two at once?

STREPS. You mean it can't?

PHEID. Of course not. Otherwise
A woman could be old and young at the same time.

STREPS. That's what the law says.

1270 PHEID. But I don't believe
That they interpret it correctly.

STREPS. Why?

PHEID. Old Solon—he was born the people's friend—

STREPS. And what's that got to do with old and new
moons?

PHEID. That's why he fixed that summonses should fall
On two days—on the last day of the old moon
And the first day of the new, so actions
Should start at the beginning of the month.

STREPS. What did he stick the old moon in for?

PHEID. So
That all the defendants should have one day

1280 To get together and settle out of court.

1259 **Attic** of Attica, the territory in which Athens stood   1272
Solon famous Athenian lawgiver c. 640-560

And if they couldn't settle, then they'd have
The first day of the month to fight it out.
   STREPS. Then why do the magistrates demand the costs
The day before, instead of on the first?
   PHEID. I guess they're responsible for public taste
And want to get their taste a day ahead.
   STREPS. Oh you poor stupid devils, sitting there
Like stones, just waiting for us clever boys
To work you over; ciphers, sheep, you heap
Of empty vessels! Things are turning out   1290
So well I feel like bursting into song
In honor of myself and sonny here—
                  [singing]
Lucky man, Strepsiades,
Born with such sharp wits as these
And possessed of such a son;
So they'll tell me every one—[breaking off]
Of my friends and fellow townsmen when they see you
Winning my cases in court; oh, they'll turn green
With envy. But you come along inside.
I want to throw a party for you first.   1300

[Exeunt STREPSIADES and PHEIDIPPIDES into the house.
      Enter PASIAS with his witness.]

   PASIAS. What! Must a man give up what belongs to him?
Not on your life! It would have been far better
To have put a bold face on it at the start
Rather than put up with this! And just
To get the money due to me, I'm forced
To bring you here to witness, and on top of that
Start a quarrel with my townsman here.
Well, I won't give my country any cause
To be ashamed of me so long as I'm
Alive. Strepsiades! I'm suing you!   1310

[Enter STREPSIADES from his house.]

   STREPS. Who is it?

1287 **Oh you . . . devils** probably addressed to the audience
1301 **Pasias** see vv. 24ff.

PAS.   You must come to court
On the last day of the old moon and the first day of the
    new.
    STREPS. I call you all to witness now: that's two days
He's talking about. Why are you suing me?
    PAS. For the five hundred that you borrowed from me
To buy the gray.
    STREPS.   The gray! Did you hear that?
Everyone here knows that I hate horses.
    PAS. God help me, you swore by the gods to pay me.
    STREPS. God help me, no I won't. Pheidippides
1320 Has learnt an argument you'll never find
An answer to.
    PAS.   You mean to say, because
Of this you're going back on what you said?
    STREPS. You bet. I'm getting something from his educa-
    tion.
    PAS. You're going to forswear it by the gods?
    STREPS. What gods?
    PAS. Zeus, Hermes and Poseidon.
    STREPS.   Yes, by Zeus,
Even if it cost five cents an oath.
This would be useful, [*poking* PASIAS *in the stomach*] if
    we rubbed it down with salt.
    PAS. You're laughing at me.
    STREPS.   It'd hold four gallons.
1330   PAS. By Zeus almighty you won't get away with this;
By all the gods you won't!
    STREPS.   The gods! That's great!
Zeus is a standing joke now with the smart set.
    PAS. Sooner or later you'll be sorry! Do you
Intend to pay or don't you? Answer me
And I'll be on my way.
    STREPS.   Hush, and I'll give you
A definite answer. Just hang on a minute. [*Exit.*]
    PAS. [*to his witness*] What do you think he'll do?
    WIT.   He'll pay all right.

[*Enter* STREPSIADES *with a breadpan.*]

1325 **Hermes** god of merchants and thieves

STREPS. Now where's that man who's asking for his
money?   **1340**
Tell me what you call this.
    PAS.   This? A pan.
    STREPS. And then you ask for money! Look at you!
I wouldn't give a cent to anyone
Who called this thing a pan. This is a pansy.
    PAS. You say that you won't pay?
    STREPS.   Not if I know it.
Come on, you pull yourself together and
Get out of here.
    PAS.   Right! Just remember this:
I'll sue you while there's breath left in my body.
    STREPS. You'll only have to pay the costs and lose
The five hundred too. I wouldn't want you to do that,
Just for being fool enough to get the pansy's name wrong.

    [*Exeunt* PASIAS *and his witness. Enter* AMYNIAS.]

    AMYNIAS. Oh dear! Oh, oh!   **1350**
    STREPS. Hey, who's that coming in here wailing? Is it
Some god or other from Carcinus' tragedies?
    AM. What? Who am I? As if you really cared!
I'm jinxed!
    STREPS. Then you can keep it to yourself.
    AM. [*in tragic manner*] O heavy fate! O Fortune, you
    have broken
My chariot wheels! O Pallas my destroyer!
    STREPS. What! Has Tlepolemus been after you?
    AM. Don't laugh at me, old boy, but tell your son
To pay me back the money that I gave him.
Things are bad, I need it more than ever.   **1360**
    STREPS. Money? What money?
    AM.   What he borrowed from me.
    STREPS. If you ask me, you really are in trouble.
    AM. I was out riding and my horses threw me.
    STREPS. You're not just off your horse, you're off your
    rocker.

1352 **Carcinus** tragic playwright frequently mocked by Aristophanes 1356 **Pallas** Athena 1357 **Tlepolemus** mythical hero represented in one of Carcinus' plays as performing some act of violence

AM. What do you mean? I only want my money back.

STREPS. You can't be quite right in the head.

AM. Who, me?

STREPS. It looks to me as if you'd been concussed.

AM. It looks to me as if you'll go to court
If you don't give me back my money!

STREPS. Tell me,
1370 What's your pet theory? When the rain comes down
Is it fresh rain every time, or does the sun
Draw up the same old rain and drop it back?

AM. I don't know, and I don't give a damn.

STREPS. And how do you expect to get your money
back
When you're so ignorant of meteorology?

AM. Well, if money's tight, at least you can
Pay me the interest.

STREPS. What's that when it's at home?

AM. What do you think? Money accumulates
And keeps on accumulating, daily, monthly,
As time goes by.
1380 STREPS. That's very nicely put.
Then do you think the sea is any bigger
Now than it used to be?

AM. No, it's just the same.
It can't get any bigger. That's not right.

STREPS. Then if it doesn't grow with all those rivers
Pouring into it, do you expect
An increase in your money? You should be ashamed!
Go on, get out of here and . . . sue yourself.
Where's my whip?

AM. Hey! I've got witnesses!

STREPS. Hanging about, eh? [striking him] Gee up, old
gray mare!

AM. This is outrageous!
1390 STREPS. Still here? Then I'll either
Flog your horse or kick your ass.
Going, are you? I thought I'd make you move—
You and your carriages and wheels and all!

[Exeunt AMYNIAS and STREPSIADES.]

CHORUS.
Look at him, lusting

After wickedness, and thrusting
His debts out of mind, impassioned to pay
Not a cent to his creditors. Mark what I say:
It's now or never;
This old man who's so clever
Will discover before the day is through   1400
He's bitten off more than he can chew.

He's got what he wanted,
A son who undaunted
Has learnt lessons well, and is set to gainsay
Any obstacle anyone puts in his way.
It's dishonest, but no matter;
It's a clever line of patter.
But for the father a time will come
When he wishes his son could be struck dumb.

[*Enter* STREPSIADES, *pursued by* PHEIDIPPIDES.]

STREPS. Ouch! Ooch!   1410
Friends and neighbors, men of this community,
Help me with all your might; I've been assaulted!
Oh my poor head, my jaw, it's agony!
You devil, do you raise your hand against your father?
   PHEID. I sure do.
   STREPS.   See, he admits it!
   PHEID.   You bet.
   STREPS. Scoundrel! Father-murderer! House-breaker!
   PHEID. You can say that again! Let's have some more!
Bad language is sweet music to my ears!
   STREPS. You fairy!
   PHEID.   Tossing me bouquets again!
   STREPS. Hit your father, would you?
   PHEID.   Yes, by Zeus; what's more,   1420
I'll prove I have just cause!
   STREPS.   God damn your impudence!
What justice could there be in beating your own father?
   PHEID. Let me explain. My logic will confound you.
   STREPS. It will, eh?
   PHEID.   With no difficulty at all.
Choose your weapons. Which argument do *you* want?
   STREPS. Which argument?

PHEID.   The better or the worse?
STREPS. By Zeus, I've really had you educated
In arguing with justice, if you're going
To prove this one—that it's upright and honest
1430 For fathers to be beaten by their sons!
PHEID. I'm pretty sure that once you've heard my proof
You'll be dumbfounded—and I do mean you!
STREPS. All right. I'd like to hear this very much
CHORUS. Old fellow, now it's up to you
    To find a way to beat your son.
    But he must have had a clue
    Or he'd never have begun.
    He's pretty sure he's going to win;
    You only have to look at him!

1440 It's necessary that you tell the chorus
Exactly how it started, and in full!
STREPS. All right, then. To begin at the beginning,
Our quarrel started thus. When I was skinning
The fatted calf, as you are well aware,
I told him bring his lyre and sing an air
Out of Simonides, "The Golden Fleecing."
And he at once replied, to sing while feasting
Was *passé*, fit for peasant women grinding wheat.
PHEID. And that was worth a beating! What—"Don't
    eat
1450 But sing!"—as if our guests were cicalas, not men!
STREPS. That's how he started—there he goes again!
And when he said Simonides lacked talent
I kept my hands off him, but wished I hadn't.
I told him to take a myrtle bough instead
And recite some Aeschylus. He shook his head
And answered "Aeschylus? That second-rater,
That ham, that bigmouth, that reverberator?"
"All right," I said—it nearly broke my heart—
"Sing us a modern song then—something smart."

1446 **Simonides** c. 556-468, lyric and elegiac poet of the old
school and so admired by Strepsiades. The poem referred to is
a punning reference to one Crius (literally "ram") who was defeated in a wrestling championship at Olympia   1455 **Aeschylus** c. 525-456 greatest tragic poet of the early Greek theatre

And he sang something from Euripides 1460
About a brother and a sister, if you please,
Having a love affair! And that was the last straw.
I called him everything, he began to roar
At me, you bet he did, and then he jumped me,
Grabbed my windpipe, booted me and thumped me—
   PHEID. You had it coming! Crying down Euripides,
That genius—
   STREPS.   If he's a genius, then you're a—[PHEIDIP-
PIDES *moves towards him.*] Please!
He's hitting me again!
   PHEID.   God knows I have good cause!
   STREPS. Aren't you ashamed? You're breaking all the
    laws.
I raised you, knew you better than you'd think;
When you were only lisping, gave you drink 1470
When you cried "Wawa!" And then when you said
"Mama!" straight away I brought you bread.
When you said "Caca!" I was on the spot
To pick you up and put you on the pot.

    And now when I'm choking
    And groaning and croaking
    You thought I was joking
    And told me to wait.
    You wanted to harry me 1480
    Rather than carry me;
    Told me to tarry-see!
    Now it's too late!

CHORUS
    Whoever here is young, his heart
    Is thumping now to hear him plead.
    How does he intend to start

1460 **Euripides** c. 485-406, dramatic poet of the new school notorious for his unorthodoxy and innovations. In his *Frogs* (405)
Aristophanes brings Euripides and Aeschylus on to the stage as
he does False and True Logic here, as exponents of the new and
old ways of life respectively   1461-2 **a brother . . . love affair**
Aristophanes professes to find this sort of sordid sensationalism
common in Euripides' tragedies

And justify his deed?
I wouldn't give, if he should win,
A fig for any old man's skin!

[*to* PHEIDIPPIDES]

1490 It's up to you now, engineer of phrases,
Word-diviner, to persuade us that you're talking honestly.

PHEID. It's great to join the *avant-garde*, to talk with
ingenuity

And argue the Establishment's compounded of fatuity.
Time was my only interest was horses—how absurd!
And every time I put three words together, then I erred!
But now he's put a stop to that, and I've been taking
lessons

In rhetoric and argument and erudite expressions,
I think that I can demonstrate it's right to beat my father.

STREPS. Go back to your horses, then, for god's sake;
for I'd rather

Pay for carriages and horses than be beaten and dis-
1500 rupted.

PHEID. Please! I'll go back to where I was before you
interrupted:

First answer me this question. Did you spank me as a
baby?

STREPS. Of course I did! I cherished you and loved you!
PHEID. That's as may be!

Then haven't I an equal right to do the selfsame thing
If, as you argue, spanking is the same as cherishing?
What! Must I put up with being knocked about, while
you

Get off without a scratch? For I was born a free man too!
If children cry, then don't you think their fathers should
cry also?

You say you have to beat sense into children? Even more
so

1510 Into old men, for they're passing into second infancy
And the older that you find them then the wiser they
should be.

So if it's right that boys should smart, their fathers should
smart harder.

STREPS. Yet I insist the law's against a boy who beats
his father!

PHEID. Who was it introduced the law? A man, like
you and me,
Who urged his wishes on the crowd, way back in history.
And is there any reason why I can't rewrite the law
So that sons can beat their fathers as their fathers did
before?
And just to show there's no ill-will, we'll give you dispen-
sation
For the blows already struck: no retroactive legislation!
Consider all the roosters and the creatures of the field: 1520
They attack their fathers, every single one of them, and
yield
In this one respect to humans: they've no legal inclination.
  STREPS. And if you're so obsessed with this, this rooster
  imitation,
Why don't you peck at farmyard dung and sleep upon a
log?
  PHEID. They aren't the same, as Socrates would tell
  you, you old dog.
  STREPS. Anyway, don't hit me, or you'll blame yourself
  some day.
  PHEID. How so?
  STREPS.   Well, if it's right for me to punish you
  this way
It's right for you to punish yours.
  PHEID.   But if I have no son
You'll die, and I'll be left with all the beating and no fun.
  STREPS. [to the audience] My friends and fellow citi-
  zens, he seems to have a case: 1530
We'll have to go along with them; it's truly a disgrace
If we do the things we shouldn't and then get away un-
punished.
  PHEID. Then look at matters this way.
  STREPS.   Any more and I'll be finished.
  PHEID. Perhaps you'll be convinced a beating isn't
  prejudicial.
  STREPS. Do you pretend to argue what I've had was
  beneficial?
  PHEID. And I'll beat my mother too!
  STREPS.   Eh? What was that? For heaven's sake!
This is getting worse than ever!
  PHEID.   Now supposing that I take

The same position in this case that I took in the other,
The weaker argument, and prove it's right to beat my
    mother?

STREPS.

1540   Supposing you do.
      Then your whole filthy crew
      And Socrates too
      Can go jump in the lake.
      False Logic as well,
      You can all go to hell.
      Oh Clouds, when I fell
      For you, what a mistake!

CHORUS. Come now, you brought it on yourself, old man,
By turning to dishonest practices.

1550   STREPS. You should have said so earlier, instead of put-
      ting
Temptation in a poor old country bumpkin's way!
    CHORUS. That's how we operate. We find a man
Enamored of disreputable courses
And lead him on until he's deep in trouble,
So he'll learn not to take the gods in vain.
    STREPS. That's hard talk, Clouds, but I've deserved it,
      every word.
It was all wrong for me to try to keep
The money that I borrowed. Dearest boy,
1560 Let's finish off that devil Chaerephon
And Socrates together, for they've cheated both of us.
    PHEID. I wouldn't want to harm my own professors.
    STREPS. You must, you must! Take thought for Zeus
      the Father!
    PHEID. You hear that? Zeus the Father? You old fool,
Is there a Zeus?
    STREPS.   There is.
    PHEID.   Of course there isn't.
Zeus has been kicked out, and Jar is king.
    STREPS. He hasn't been kicked out. That was where I
      went wrong
On account of this Jar. Oh, what an idiot I was,
Believing that a piece of crockery was god!
    PHEID. You're crazy. But go on, talk nonsense to your-
      self. [*Exit.*]

STREPS. Mad, mad, mad! I must have lost my mind   1570
To jettison the god because of Socrates.
But Hermes, as you love me, don't be angry with me now
Or work my undoing; forgive me my offenses;
It was all that talking that unsettled me.
Give me advice. Would it be better for me
To pester them with lawsuits—or what do you think?
[*pretending to listen*]
Don't go to law. That's excellent advice.
Don't waste a moment, but burn down the house
These talking fools inhabit.
[*calling to his slave*]   Here, here, Xanthias!
Come on, bring your ladder and your pitchfork with you.   1580
Then climb on to the roof of Highbrow Hall
And lever off the tiles, if you love your master,
Until you've brought the house down round their ears.
And someone bring a torch, a lighted one—
I'll take my vengeance on the lot of them today.
Let's hear if they can talk themselves out of this!

[*The slaves appear with ladders, spades, forks and torches;*
STREPSIADES *mounts the roof and sets fire to the Academy,*
and the students are heard shouting, first inside and then
in full view of the audience as, with SOCRATES, *they*
scramble desperately out of the blazing building.]

STUDENT. Help, help!
STREPS. Fire away, torch, that's what I brought you
    for!
STUD. Hey there! What are you doing?
STREPS. What do you think I'm doing? I'm conducting   1590
Research in depth into your roof!
STUD. Who's burning down our house?
STREPS. The man you stole the cloak from!
STUD. Murder! Murder!
STREPS. That's exactly what I have in mind, unless
This pickaxe should betray my expectations
Or I should fall down there and break my neck!
SOC. You, sir, on the roof! What are you doing?
STREPS. Walking on air, and looking at the sun!
SOC. Help me! I'm suffocating! What shall I do?   1600
STUD. Hey, this is murder! I'll be roasted alive!

STREPS. This will teach you to insult the gods
And peek into the houses of the moon.
[*to his slaves*]
Punch them, whack them, don't let them get away;
They've got it coming, most of all because—
And you know why—they blasphemed against the gods!
CHORUS. Let us exit, singing, dancing; that's enough for
one day.

THE POT OF GOLD

(Aulularia)

❧

Plautus

CHARACTERS

❧

The Household God of EUCLIO, *speaker of the Prologue.*
EUCLIO ("Goodname") *a miserly old man.*
STAPHYLA ("Grape") *an old woman, his slave.*
EUNOMIA ("Tidy") *a wealthy lady, sister of* MEGADORUS.
MEGADORUS ("Squire Bountiful") *a wealthy middle-aged man.*
PYTHODICUS ("His Master's Voice") *head slave of* MEGA-
DORUS' *household.*
CONGRIO ("Eel")
ANTHRAX ("Coal") } *slave cooks in* MEGADORUS' *household*
STROBILUS ("Spinning Top") *slave to* LYCONIDES.
LYCONIDES, *a smart young gentleman, son of* EUNOMIA.
PHAEDRIA *daughter of* EUCLIO (*heard only as a voice off-
stage.*)
PHRYGIA *and* ELEUSIUM, *music girls; other slaves.*

Roman plays retained much of the local color of the
Greek originals from which they were translated, and so
the setting is probably intended to be Athens. However,
for practical purposes it might as well be Rome, or indeed
any Mediterranean city of the Greco-Roman period. The
scene represents a street with three buildings: the house
of MEGADORUS, impressive and ornate; the house of EUCLIO
next door, poor and shabby but still clean; and the Shrine
of Faith. Near the buildings stands an outdoor altar.
Alleyways lead between the houses and offstage in various
directions—to the forum, to other parts of the city, and
outside the city walls.

THE POT OF GOLD

FIRST ARGUMENT

Old miser Euclio, who barely trusts himself,
Digs up a pot that's buried in his house
And full of gold. He puts its back at once
And goes half crazy watching it. Lyconides
Has wronged the miser's daughter; and old Megadorus,
Persuaded by his sister to get married,
Asks for the daughter as his wife.
The old man gives his grudging promise. Fearing
For his gold, he takes it from his home and hides it
In one place, then another; but he's spied on
By the servant of that same Lyconides
Who dishonored his daughter, and who now implores
His uncle Megadorus to give him the girl
Because he loves her. Not long after, Euclio
Is tricked out of his gold, and thinks it's gone
For ever. When he gets it back again
He's thrilled, and gives Lyconides his daughter.

SECOND ARGUMENT

After he's found a pot of treasure, Euclio
Uses his energy in anxious watching.
Lyconides has ravished Euclio's daughter;
Uncle Megadorus wants to marry her undowried,
Lending his cooks to make the wedding breakfast.
Afraid for his treasure's safety, Euclio
Removes it from home, and the seducer's slave
Investigates and steals it. The boy tells all
And ends up with the gold, girl and the baby.

Although the metrical Arguments, or plot-summaries, postdate
the play, they are included here for their interest and also for
their importance in reconstructing the play's ending. The Second Argument is in acrostic form, with the first letter of each
line spelling the Latin title of the play.

PROLOGUE

spoken by EUCLIO's *Household God*

In case somebody's wondering, I'll briefly
Introduce myself: I am the Household God
Belonging to the family you saw me leaving.
I've kept a watchful and proprietary eye
On this establishment for many years now,
For the father of the present occupant
And his before him. This man's grandfather
Begged my assistance and entrusted me with gold,
A treasure no one knew about. He buried it
10 In the middle of the fireplace, offering a prayer
To me to keep it safe. And when he died—
Old miser that he was—he'd no intention
Of telling his own son its whereabouts
But chose to leave him to a life of poverty
Rather than show him where the treasure was.
All he bequeathed him was a tiny acreage
On which he sweated for a meager living.
When he passed on—the one who pledged his gold with
     me—
I began to watch the son, to see if he
20 Would rate me higher than his father had.
But he cared less and less for me, and gave me
Still smaller share of honor. I gave him
As good as he deserved, and he too passed away,
Leaving as issue the son who now
Lives in this house, a fellow of the same
Stamp as his father and his grandfather.
He has one daughter. Every day she comes
To pay her respects, and always has
A pinch of incense for me, or some wine—
30 Something, anyway—and hangs me round with garlands.
Out of gratitude for her deserving, I've contrived
That Euclio should discover this same treasure,

Household God the Roman *lar familiaris,* benevolent domestic
spirit who supervised the household and its affairs and whose
shrine customarily stood within private houses

So he can find her a husband, if he wants to,
More easily—because a boy
From one of the best families has raped her.
The boy knows who the girl was that he ravished,
But she doesn't know him, nor does her father
Know what's happened to her. This day I'll arrange it
So the old gentleman who lives next door
Will ask for her in marriage. That way I'll   40
Contrive it so the boy who ravished her
Can marry her more easily—the old man
Who'll ask for her in marriage is the uncle
Of the boy who at the all-night Festival of Ceres
Forced himself on her. But here's the old fellow
Raising the roof as always, driving his old woman
Out in the street, so she won't know
What's going on. I guess he has a mind to look
At his gold, and see nobody's stolen it.

EUCLIO. [*offstage*] Out, do you hear, get out! This is
    where you belong,   50
Outside! You female spy, your eyes are always
Out on business!

[*Enter* STAPHYLA *from* EUCLIO's *house, followed by* EUCLIO
who is pushing and beating her.]

STAPHYLA.   Oh, the life I lead!
What am I being beaten for?
    EUC.   To make you
Suffer, you old witch, and give you
The hard time you deserve.
    STAPH.   What have you pushed me
Out of the house for?
    EUC.   Do I owe you any explanations,
You punching bag? Don't stand there by the door!
Come over here!

[STAPHYLA *hobbles in his direction.*]

       Just look at that, the way she's walking!
Do you know what I'd like to do to you?
By god, if I could only get my hands   60

44 **Ceres** goddess of crops

On a bullwhip or a club this very minute
I'd put some snap into that tortoise pace of yours.
    STAPH. I wish to heaven I could hang myself.
Far better that than slave for you this way.
    EUC. Just listen how she's mumbling to herself,
The bitch! I'll tear out those sharp eyes of yours,
You devil, so you can't keep tabs on me.
Move over there a bit. Keep moving. Further. Right!
You stay right there. If you so much as move
70 One finger's width, one nail's breadth from that spot
Or look around until I give the word,
By god, I'll give you a lesson! I'll string you up
Then and there. [*aside*] One thing I know for sure, I've
     never
Seen a more desperate character than this old woman.
I'm terrified she'll find some sneaky way
To catch me unawares, and ferret out
My buried gold. Goddamn her, she has eyes
In the back of her head. Now I'll go in and see
If the gold is where I left it. Since I found it
80 I haven't had a single easy moment. [*Exit to his house.*]
    STAPH. God be my witness, I have no idea
What's got into my master, or what makes him so
Demented. That's the story of my life—
Ten times a day he throws me out of doors.
He's half out of his mind, and god knows why.
He lies awake all night, and in the daytime
He's like a crippled cobbler, sitting home all day.
And how I can cover up his daughter's shame
I wish I knew—the baby's on the way,
90 It's any day now. Best thing I can do,
I guess, is knot myself a noose among
The beams, and with my body write long I.

[EUCLIO *reappears from his house.*]

    EUC. That's one worry over. I can come outdoors
Now I've seen that everything's safe and sound inside.
Here, you! Go in again and keep an eye
On everything indoors.

92 **long I** her thin body dangling from the rope would resemble
this letter

STAPH.   Indoors, indeed!
Are you afraid someone'll steal the house?
There's nothing else a thief could get away with—
The place is full of emptiness and cobwebs.
    EUC. Well, well! I should have been born King Darius, 100
Or Philip, I suppose, just for your benefit,
You poisonous old witch. If there are cobwebs,
They're my cobwebs, and I want them watched.
I haven't any money; I admit it and
Submit to it. I take what heaven sends me.
Go in and lock the door behind you. I'll be back directly.
And if I catch you letting strangers in . . .
They might come asking for a light, so put the fires out,
Then they'll have no reason to come asking for you;
And if that fire stays in, I'll put you out!   110
If anyone comes asking for a drink, you tell him
We've run clear out of water. If he wants a knife,
A chopper, pestle, mortar, or the pots
The neighbors always borrow, then you tell him
That we had burglars, everything's been stolen.
While I'm away, I want no living soul
Let in this house. You mark my words,
If Dame Fortune comes in person, don't admit her.
    STAPH. I guess you can leave that to her. She's never
Come within a mile of us before.   120
    EUC. Get in and shut your mouth.
    STAPH.   I'm shutting it. Goodbye.
    EUC. And double-bolt the door. I'll be straight back.

[*Exit* STAPHYLA *to the house, closing the door behind her.*]

I have to go out, and it's tearing me apart.
I've never wanted to go less. But all the same
I know what I'm doing. Our precinct chairman
Announced a handout—every man one silver piece.
If I pass it up and don't go after it
They're all bound to suspect immediately
I have some gold at home; it isn't like

100 **Darius** name of several kings of fabulously wealthy Persia
101 **Philip** of Macedon in Greece, father of Alexander the Great
125-6 **Our precinct chairman . . . silver piece** such distributions of money, made through the regular electoral divisions of the city, became increasingly familiar in Roman society

130 A pauper not to take a little bit of trouble
To get a silver piece. The way things are,
When I'm so careful to conceal my secret
From everybody, I keep thinking that the whole world
    knows,
And that people are a lot more glad to see me
Than they used to be; they stop and visit with me,
They shake me by the hand, they keep on asking
"How are you feeling?" "How are things?" "How's it
    going?"
Well, I'll be going on my errand now,
And hurry back as quickly as I can.

[*Exit* EUCLIO, *in the direction of town. Enter* EUNOMIA
and MEGADORUS *from the latter's house.*]

140   EUNOMIA. Brother, I hope that you'll believe
That what I say is prompted by my conscience
And your well-being; as your sister born
I can do no less. I'm well aware
What people say of us—we're busybodies,
Chatterboxes; if the cap fits, wear it.
They say there's never been a woman yet
Who could hold her tongue. But that's as may be.
However, brother, do keep this in mind,
That I'm your closest relative and *vice versa*,
150 And so it's only proper we should give each other
Advice and encouragement, when we see
Something affecting the other's well-being.
We mustn't have secrets from each other
Or be afraid of speaking our minds.
What's mine must be yours as yours is mine.
That's why I've brought you outdoors privately
For a heart-to-heart talk about family matters.
    MEGADORUS. Sister, you're perfect. Give me your hand
    EUN. [*coyly*] Perfect? Why, who *can* you mean?
    MEG. You.
    EUN.   You don't say so.
160   MEG.   Not if you don't.
    EUN. No, it's only fair to tell the truth.
It isn't right to rank one woman best;
It's just that some aren't quite as good as others.
    MEG. That's exactly my opinion too.

That's one thing, sister, that we'll never fight about.

EUN. Now, be a good boy and pay attention.

MEG. I'm all ears, at your disposal.
Your slightest wish is my command.

EUN. Well, I've come to give you some advice
On something I consider very good for you—   170

MEG. That's so like you, sister.

EUN.   I should hope so.

MEG. Well, what is it?

EUN.   Something that would give you
Lasting security. You should have children—

MEG. I should be so lucky!

EUN.   And so I want you
To find yourself a wife.

MEG.   That's murderous!

EUN. What?

MEG.   Sister, when you talk that way
You might as well be knocking out my brains.
Every word's a millstone round my neck.

EUN. Do as your sister says.

MEG.   I would,
If I could only do it with a smile.   180

EUN. It's for your own good.

MEG.   Marry? I'd die rather.
But I'll marry, if you like, on this condition—
Wedding tomorrow, and the next day out she goes
Feet first. Accept my terms? Then bring her on,
And sound the wedding bells.

EUN. Brother, I can marry you to somebody
Who'd bring you in a fortune. But
She's not exactly young; in fact, the lady's
Middle-aged. But at a word from you
I'll tell her that you're asking for her hand.   190

MEG. May I ask a question?

EUN.   Anything you like.

MEG. When a man the wrong side of middle age him-
    self
Marries a middle-aged woman—just supposing
He manages to get the old girl pregnant,
What do you bet that when the boy is born
He'll just have time to see his dad pass out?
Sister, I'll shoulder the responsibility

And make it easy for you. Thanks be to the gods
And to our ancestors, I'm rich enough.
200 These great heiresses with their haughty ways,
Enormous dowries, shouting for attention,
Their carriages with ivory appointments,
Their wardrobes, their magnificent regalia,
They leave me cold. Such things make slaves
Out of the men who have to pay for them.
    EUN. Who will you marry, then?
    MEG.   I'll tell you.
You know old Euclio next door, without
A penny to his name?
    EUN.   Yes. He's respectable.
    MEG. It's his daughter that I want to marry.
210 Save your breath, sister. I know what you're going
To say. She hasn't any money. Well,
That's exactly what I like about her.
    EUN. I hope that you'll be happy.
    MEG.   So do I.
    EUN. Well, if there's nothing I can do . . .
    MEG.   Take care.
    EUN. And you.   [Exit.]
    MEG.   I'll go and see if Euclio's at home.
Oh, here he is. He must have just come back.

[Enter EUCLIO, grumbling to himself.]

    EUC. When I was going out I had an intuition
It was a waste of time. That's why I didn't
Feel like going. Not one man from the precinct
220 Turned up, nor yet the chairman, though it was his job
To share out the money. Now I can't get home fast
    enough.
My body's here, but home is where the heart is.
    MEG. [accosting him] A long life and good fortune to
    you, Euclio!
    EUC. God bless you, Megadorus.
    MEG.   Well, how are you?
Is everything going as well as you could wish?
    EUC. [aside] When a rich man talks politely to a poor
    man
He's up to something. This man knows about my gold.
And that's the reason for this extra civil greeting.

MEG. Well, what's the word? How are you doing? Fine?
EUC. Things could be a whole lot better moneywise.   230
MEG. As long as you don't let things get you down,
That's all you need to lead a decent life.
    EUC. [*aside*] The old bag told him of my gold, it's clear
    as daylight.
Ooh, I'll cut out her tongue, I'll tear her eyes out
When I get home.
    MEG.   What are you muttering about?
    EUC. How miserable it is to have no money.
I have a grownup daughter with no dowry—
Can't get her off my hands, can't find a man
To look at her.
    MEG.   Shush, shush. You don't have a thing
To worry about. I'll use my influence to see   240
She gets a husband, Euclio. If there's anything you need,
Just say the word.
    EUC. [*aside*]   He's offering to help.
He's after something. It's my gold, he's drooling for it.
He gives a crust with one hand, and the other holds
A stone behind his back. I never trust
A rich man when he butters up a poor one.
He pats you on the back and squashes you.
Oh, I know them. When once they've got their tentacles
    around you
They never let you go.
    MEG.   Er, Euclio,
Can I trouble you for a minute of your time?   250
I have a proposition that I want to put to you;
It's in our common interest—
    EUC. [*aside*]   Good grief!
He's got his claws into my gold, and now he wants
To split with me. I'll take a sneaky look indoors.

        [*He moves towards his house.*]

    MEG. Where are you going?
    EUC.   I'll be back with you directly—
There's something that I have to do indoors—   [*Exit.*]
    MEG. You know, I think that when I talk about his
    daughter
And say I want to marry her, he'll think
I'm laughing at him. He's so sensitive

260 About his poverty, he won't let anything get past him.

[EUCLIO *reappears from his house.*]

EUC. [*aside*] The gods are good to me, I'm safe—if it's
all there.
I was scared stiff. I nearly passed out on the doorstep.
[*aloud*] Well, Megadorus, here I am again.
What was it?

MEG.   Thanks, it's very kind of you.
I'm going to ask you . . . please don't be offended . . .

EUC. As long as you say nothing to annoy me.

MEG. What's your opinion of my family?

EUC.   It's good.

MEG. My credit rating?

EUC.   Good.

MEG.   My personal behavior?

EUC. Impeccable.

MEG.   You know my age?

270 EUC. A tidy figure, like your bank account.

MEG. And I've always known you for a freeman of this
city
Without a stain upon your name, and have no reason
To change my mind.

EUC. [*aside*]   He's sniffing at my gold.
[*aloud*] All right. What are you after?

MEG.   Now we know each other,
Something I hope will be to my advantage
And yours to, and your daughter's. I'm requesting
Your daughter's hand in marriage. Please consent.

EUC. Oh, Megadorus! It's unworthy of a man
In your position to make fun of me.

280 I can't defend myself. I've never
Harmed you or yours. What have I ever said
Or done to give you an excuse to treat me so?

MEG. I'm not laughing at you. That's not what I came
for.
I wouldn't think of such a thing.

EUC.   Then what's all this
About my daughter?

MEG.   I just want to help you out
And let you and your family help me.

EUC. You want to know what I think, Megadorus?

You're rich, with a position in society.
I'm poor—the poorest man you ever saw.
If I gave you my daughter, this is what I think: 290
You'd be the ox, and I should be the ass.
If we teamed up, I couldn't pull my weight;
Down goes ass in the mud, and for all the attention
I'd get from you, friend ox, I might as well
Never have been born. It would be too one-sided,
And my own sort would laugh at me. If anything
Should come between us, then I wouldn't have a place
To call my own, in your world or in mine.
The asses would chew me into little pieces,
The oxen run at me and gore me. That's the risk   300
You run, if you're an ass with ox ambitions.

MEG. The closer you can get to honorable connections
The better off you are. Accept my proposition
And let me marry her.

EUC.   I can't give any dowry.

MEG. Then don't. As long as she's been well brought up
She has sufficient dowry and to spare.

EUC. Don't you go thinking that I've found a treasure,
    now!

MEG. I know it. There's no need to keep on telling me.
Say yes to our engagement.

EUC.   Very well. [*jumping*] Good god,
I'm ruined!

MEG.   What's the matter?

EUC.   What's that clinking noise?   310

MEG. I'm having my garden dug—

        [EUCLIO *rushes into his house.*]

                    Now where's he gone?
Run off and left me waiting for an answer!
Because he sees I'm trying to make friends
He thinks that he's too good for me. That's human nature.
When a rich man makes advances to a poor one
The poor man is afraid to come half way
And in his nervousness he lets the chance slip by.
Then, when his opportunity has vanished,
He'd give anything to have it back again.

[EUCLIO *reenters from his house, shouting to* STAPHYLA
                within.]

320 EUC. By god, if I don't have your tongue torn out
By the roots, I give you my unqualified permission
To make a eunuch of me!

MEG. Well, well, Euclio!
I see you think that I'm the sort of man
To be made a fool of—at my time of life,
And when I haven't given you the slightest cause!

EUC. Why, Megadorus, that's not what I'm doing.
I couldn't even if I wanted to.

MEG. Well, are you giving me your daughter's hand?

EUC. All right—but only under the conditions
330 And with the dowry that I mentioned earlier.

MEG. Can we get married, then?

EUC. All right, you can.

MEG. May heaven bless our union!

EUC. I hope so.
But you remember what we just agreed
About the dowry; she won't have one penny.

MEG. Yes, I remember.

EUC. See, I know your sort
And how you like to keep things in the air—
It's on, it's off again, it's off, it's on,
As the fancy takes you.

MEG. Well, there'll be no cause
For us to quarrel. Is there any reason
Why the marriage can't take place today?

340 EUC. No reason
In the world, that I know of.

MEG. Then I'll be going
And get things ready. Sure there's nothing else?

EUC. That's all. You go now, and good luck to you.

MEG. [shouting] Hey, Pythodicus, on the double! Get
Behind me, do you hear, we're going shopping!

[Enter PYTHODICUS from MEGADORUS' house; exeunt PY-
THODICUS and MEGADORUS to the market place.]

EUC. Well, there he goes. Immortal gods, I ask you,
The things that money can do! His tongue is hanging out
    for it,

330 the dowry . . . earlier i.e. none at all

And that's why he's so set on marrying my daughter.
[*going to the door of his house and calling*]
Where are you, blabbermouth? So the whole neighbour-
   hood
Knows that my daughter has a dowry! Hey, Staphyla!   350
Have you gone deaf?

[*Enter* STAPHYLA.]

                      Get busy, wash the dinner service.
My daughter's engaged! Today she marries Megadorus.
   STAPH. God bless us all! She can't, it's all too sudden.
   EUC. Shut your mouth and get indoors. See everything's
      done
When I get back from market. Lock the door behind you.
I'll be straight back.

[*Exit to the market place.*]

   STAPH.   Now what am I to do?
We're as good as finished, me and missy both.
It's almost time for the kid and the disgrace
To make their appearance. We've managed to keep it
   dark
So far, but there's no hiding any longer.   360
Well, in we go, so master will find things
The way he wanted them. Oh, deary me,
I shall drink trouble laced with tears today!

[*Exit* STAPHYLA *into the house. Enter, from the market-
place,* PYTHODICUS *with the two cooks* ANTHRAX *and*
CONGRIO, *the flute-girls* PHRYGIA *and* ELEUSIUM, *and a
number of other slaves with provisions from the market,
among them two lambs.*]

   PYTHODICUS. After master had gone shopping, he
Hired these cooks and flute-girls at the forum
And instructed me to split the lot two ways.
   ANTHRAX. Let me tell you, nobody's splitting me two
      ways.
[*sniggering*] But if you want to go the whole way, I'm
   your man!
   CONGRIO. Well, quite the lady, aren't we, pretty boy?
You wouldn't let them get between you, eh?   370

PYTH. Now, Anthrax, that's not what I meant,
And well you know it. Listen. My master's getting
Married today.

ANTH.   Who's the lucky girl?

PYTH. The daughter of old Euclio next door.
The orders are that he gets half the food,
One of the cooks, and one flute-girl as well.

ANTH. You mean half stays, and half goes home to your
     place?

PYTH. You said it.

ANTH.   Couldn't the old boy afford
To pay for his own daughter's wedding breakfast?

PYTH. Huh!

ANTH.   What's all that about?

380   PYTH.   You need to ask?
It's easier squeezing blood out of a stone
Than squeezing him.

ANTH.   No!

CONG.   You don't say!

PYTH.   Well, work it
Out for yourself; if a fly lights on his plate
He thinks he's heading straight for bankruptcy.
And that's not all. If a wisp of smoke gets through
His walls into the street, he goes round shouting:
"Immortal gods! Is there no justice in this world!"
And that's not all. Before he goes to bed
He ties a bag around his neck.

ANTH.   Why's that?

PYTH. So he won't lose any breath while he's asleep.

ANTH. Why doesn't he plug up his windpipe at the
390   other end
So he won't lose any wind while he's asleep?

PYTH. Believe you me, if you believe my stories
Then I'll believe yours.

ANTH.   Oh, I do believe you,
Indeed I do.

PYTH.   And you know something else?
He cries when he throws out his washing water.

ANTH. Well, what do you think our chances are
Of getting five hundred out of this old boy
That we can use to buy our freedom with?

PYTH. If you asked him for starvation as a loan

He wouldn't give it you. The other day   400
He got himself a manicure, and you know what he said?
"Wrap up the clippings, and I'll take them home."
    ANTH. That's a miser if I ever heard one.
    PYTH. You haven't heard anything yet. The other day
A buzzard flew off with a piece of meat of his.
Off to the jail he runs, it was pitiful to see him—
He weeps, he yells, he screams "Arrest that bird!
I'm suing him for petty larceny!"
There are a thousand stories I could tell
If we had time. Come on, now. Which of you is faster?   410
    ANTH. Me. No comparison.
    PYTH.   I'm talking about cooking,
Not stealing.
    ANTH.   Cooking's what I meant.
    PYTH. What about you?
    CONG.   I'm just the way I look.
    ANTH. Oh, he's a weekend cook, he only comes
To work one day in seven.
    CONG.   You five-letter man,
T-H-I-E-F, thief! Who do you think
You're talking to?
    ANTH.   Yah, thief yourself. You and your letters!
You know where they belong—back in the pen!
    PYTH. You shut your mouth. Pick out the fattest lamb,
        and take it
Back to our place.
    ANTH.   Right you are. [*Exit to* MEGADORUS' *house.*]
    PYTH.   And Congrio,   420
Pick up the one he's left, and take it
[*pointing to* EUCLIO's *house*]   To that house over there.
[*to some of the attendants*] You go along with him.
The rest of you, come over here to our place.
    CONG.   Hey!
It's not fair shares! They get the fattest lamb!
    PYTH. Then you can have the fattest dancing girl.
Yes, Phrygia, off you go. Eleusium,
You can come home with us.

[*Exeunt* ELEUSIUM *and others into the house of* MEGA-
                        DORUS]

    CONG. Hey, Pythodicus, you're a crafty one.

Pushing me off on this old pennypincher.
430 If I want something here, I'll have to
Shout myself hoarse before I get it.

    PYTH. Oh, you're an idiot. What's the percentage
In being honest, when there's not a thing
To be got out of it?

    CONG.   You don't say?

    PYTH.   Yes, I do say.
In the first place, once you've gone inside that door
You'll be all on your lonesome. If there's anything you
    want
Take it from home, don't waste time asking for it.
There's always an enormous crowd at our place,
Furniture, gold, clothes, silver plate;
440 If anything's missing there—I know it's easier
To keep your hands off when there's nothing going—
They can say "The cooks have stolen it, arrest them,
Tie them up, thrash them, throw them in the dungeon."
You'll miss all this; you won't have anything to steal
Where you are. Come along.

    CONG.   All right, I'm coming.

    [PYTHODICUS *leads the way to* EUCLIO's *house.*]

    PYTH. [*knocking*] Hey, come on, Staphyla, open up.
    STAPH. [*within*]   Who is it?
    PYTH. Pythodicus.
    STAPH. [*opening the door and looking out*] What do
    you want?
    PYTH.   Take delivery:
These cooks, one flute-girl and some groceries
For the wedding breakfast. Megadorus said
They were to go to Euclio.
450   STAPH.   Hey, Pythodicus,
What are we celebrating? Total abstinence?

    PYTH. Why?

    STAPH.   I don't notice any booze around.

    PYTH. It'll come directly, when Himself gets back
From the forum.

    STAPH.   There's no firewood in the house.

    CONG. Don't you have any rafters?

    STAPH.   Yes, of course.

    CONG. Then don't go out, there's firewood in the house.

STAPH. Why, you dirty— you may be a firebug,
But do you think I'm going to burn the house down
To cook your dinner or to save your pocket?
　　CONG. It never crossed my mind.
　　PYTH.　　　　　　　　　Right, take 'em in.
　　STAPH.　　　　　　　　　　　Come on.　460

[*Exeunt* STAPHYLA, CONGRIO, PHRYGIA *and the other slaves
into* EUCLIO's *house.*]

　　PYTH. [*calling after them*] Take care of things! I'll go
　　　and see what's cooking.
[*walking over to* MEGADORUS' *house*]
I'm going crazy keeping an eye on them.
There's only one solution—put them in the dungeon
To cook, and we can hoist the courses up on baskets.
But what they cooked down there they'd eat themselves.
Downstairs would dine, and upstairs would go hungry.
But here I stand talking, as if there weren't enough to
　　do
With all those sons of robbers in the house.

[*Exit into* MEGADORUS' *house. Enter* EUCLIO *from the market place, carrying a small parcel and a few flowers.*]

　　EUC. When it came to the point, I wanted to make
　　　certain
I'd be in good shape for my daughter's wedding.　470
I go to market, and I ask to see some fish.
They show me some. The fish is dear. Lamb's dear,
Beef's dear, so's veal, so's pork and so is seafood.
Everything's dear—and all the dearer when
You haven't any money anyway.
I lost my temper when I couldn't buy
And walked home emptyhanded. That'll teach the scum.
Then on the way home I began to think
Things over—squander on a holiday,
Want on a working day, if you're not careful.　480
After I put this proposition to my heart
And stomach, reason seconded the motion,
To wit, that I should marry off my daughter
At minimum expense. And so I bought
This pinch of frankincense, and this bouquet.
They'll do to dress the altar of our household god

To make him give his blessing to my daughter's wedding.
[*looking towards his house*]
What in the world is this? My door's wide open,
And there's a noise inside. Help! It's a holdup!
490   CONG. [*within*] Go ask the neighbors for a bigger pot
If they have one; this doesn't hold enough.
   EUC. Death and damnation! My money's good as gone,
They're looking for the pot. If I don't get
Inside there fast, I might as well give up the ghost.
Apollo, help me and protect me, I beseech you!
Stick them full of arrows, these bank-robbers,
If ever you've helped at times like these before!
What am I waiting for? My money or my life!

[*He plunges into the house. Enter* ANTHRAX *from* MEGA-
DORUS' *house, shouting to the slaves inside.*]

   ANTH. Dromo, you clean the fish. Machaerio,
500   Fillet the eel and lamprey. Do the best you can.
I'll run next door to beg a baking pan
From Congrio. And if you know what's good for you
You'll pluck that rooster smoother than a chorus boy
Before you give it back to me. Hey, what's that ruckus
Coming from next door? Oh, it's the cooks, I guess.
They're only doing what comes naturally.
I'll get inside, before they riot here.

[CONGRIO *and his fellow slaves tumble out of* EUCLIO's
house, shouting and crying.]

   CONG. Help! Help! Friends, Romans, countrymen
And anybody else's countrymen, make way,
510   Give me room to run, keep off, clear the streets!
It's the first time I cooked in a crazy house!
They gave me—ouch!—and my helpers such
A drubbing with their sticks I ache all over.
I'm fit to die, after the old man's finished
Taking me for his gymnasium.
O misery! I give up the ghost!
He's opening the crazy house, he's coming
After me. I know very well
What'll happen to me now—I've had
520   Good lessons from my master. Never in this world
Have I seen anybody who could handle

A stick so neatly; he beat us all
Into the ground, and kicked us out.

    EUC. [*emerging from the house*] Stop, thief! Stay where
        you are!

    CONG.   What are you shouting at?
You idiot?

    EUC.   I'll go right down to the courthouse
And turn you in.

    CONG.   What for?

    EUC.   For carrying a knife!

    CONG. Cooks have to carry knives!

    EUC.   And uttering menaces!

    CONG. You're right, I should have had more sense.
I should have stuck you with it.

    EUC.   You're a menace to society!
And if there's anything else that I can do   530
To hurt you, all you have to do is name it.

    CONG. Don't rub it in. You made that clear already.
Just look at me. You're beaten me so hard
I've got a skin as soft as any fruit.
Why did you rough us up, old miser?

    EUC.   Why?
You still ask? It's no less than you deserved.

    CONG. Now cut that out! If I'm smart you'll rot in hell.

    EUC. We'll see about that. I've made you smart, all right!
What business did you have inside my house
When I was out, without my orders? Answer me!   540

    CONG. Well, you can just keep quiet and I'll tell you.
To cook for the wedding.

    EUC.   What's it got to do with you,
You devil, if I eat cooked meals or have them raw?
Who do you think you are, my nanny?

    CONG.   Answer me
One question. Will you let us in your house
To cook dinner, or will you not?

    EUC.   You answer me
One question: will my property be safe
In my own home?

    CONG.   The only thing I want
Is to get out of here with all my property
As sound as when I brought it. My stuff's good enough   550
For me—I don't want anything of yours.

EUC. All right, I know it, you don't have to tell me.

CONG. What do you want to stop us cooking dinner for?

What have we said or done that you don't like?

EUC. You still ask that, you villain, when you've turned my rooms

And every corner of my house into a throughway?

If you'd stayed in the kitchen where you had business to be,

You'd have a whole head now. It's all your fault.

All right, then, if you want to know my mind:

560 If you come one step closer to this door without my orders

There isn't any man alive who'd be in your shoes

After I've finished with you. Now you know my mind.

[EUCLIO *goes back into his house and slams the door.*]

CONG. Where are you going now? Hey! You come back here!

So help me Holy Mother of the thieving classes,

If you don't tell them to give back my pots

I'll sit here on your doorstep all night long

And tear your reputation into little pieces.

Now what? By gosh, somebody's put the jinx on this job.

I'm not paid worth a dime, and now I've got

570 A doctor's bill besides.

[EUCLIO *emerges from his house with the pot of gold hidden under his cloak.*]

EUC. [*aside*] I'll take this everywhere I go, and keep it with me.

I'll never leave it there again. Why, anything

Might happen. [*to* CONGRIO] Now you can go in, the lot of you—

Cooks, flute-girls—take the whole rogue's gallery along

If it amuses you. Work, cook, make hay, do your worst.

CONG. About time too, when you've just smashed my head in.

EUC. Get in with you. You're paid to work, not talk.

CONG. Listen, old man. I want some compensation for my beating.

I'm paid to cook a dinner, not be knocked about.

580 EUC. Then go ahead and sue me. Boy, you bother me.

Go cook the dinner—or else get out of here
And hang yourself.
    CONG.   And you can go and—
                [*Exit into house.*]
    EUC. He's gone. O gods in heaven! When a poor man
Does any sort of business with a rich one
He starts more than he knows. Here's Megadorus
Getting round me every which way till I'm dizzy,
Pretending he sent me these cooks as a compliment.
He can't fool me. They came here to steal *this*.
[*fondling his pot*]
And that rooster—the one that my old woman had—
Was every bit as bad. He nearly ruined me;   590
He started scratching round the corner where this pot
Was buried. I had heart-failure, I needn't tell you;
I grabbed a stick and broke that rooster's neck
Caught in the act, the thief! I wouldn't be surprised
If those cooks hadn't promised the rooster a cut
For informing. Well, I've pulled the rug from under them.
No need to say another word. And as for mister rooster
There's no fight left in him

      [MEGADORUS *appears from the market place.*]

                    But here comes neighbor
Megadorus from the forum. I don't have the nerve
To pass him without stopping for a chat.   600

[EUCLIO *withdraws to one side.* MEGADORUS *talks to himself.*]

    MEG. I told a number of my friends about
My wedding plans. They were delighted.
"Euclio's daughter's a lovely girl,"
They said, "You couldn't have made a better choice."
It's my opinion that if all our richer citizens
Followed my lead, and married girls
Out of the poorer families, without a dowry,
There'd be more concord in the body politic,
We wouldn't be so keen to spite each other,
Our women would be more afraid of trouble,   610
And we should see the cost of living fall.
Yes, that'd be best for nearly everyone.
But there's always a minority of troublemakers

Who only see what's in it for themselves,
So greedy and impossible to satisfy,
That neither law of land nor rule of thumb
Can take their measure. And if anybody says
"Who will the rich girls marry, then,
The ones with dowries, if this poor-law passes?"
620 They can marry whom they please, always providing
Their dowry doesn't go along with them. If things
Were done this way, our girls would see to it
That they provide themselves with better dispositions
Than they have now; and that would be their dowry!
The way things are now, fancy carriage mules will fetch
A bigger price than thoroughbreds. But if I had my way,
They'd sell cheaper than imported third-rate packhorses.
    EUC. [*aside*] God bless me, it's a joy to listen to the man
Deliver such a brilliant sermon on economy.
630   MEG. Then she can never say "I brought you a dowry
Bigger than anything you could scrape together!
And so it's no more than I'm entitled to
To have gold and purple, maids to wait on me,
Mules and their drivers, running footmen,
Boys to run errands, and a carriage I can ride in."
    EUC. [*aside*] Tremendous! He knows women inside out!
I wish they'd make him Minister of Feminine Deportment!
    MEG. Wherever you go these days, you see more car-
       riages
In city streets than working in the country.
640 But that's a joy compared to when they come for money.
There stands the cleaner, there the jeweler,
Modes in Knitwear and the Trinket Shop,
Peddlers of laces, lingerie makers,
Dyers of flame-pink, mauve and cerise,
Sellers of sleeves and scented slippers,
Linen dealers, toe-and-heelers,
Makers of mules for milady's boudoir;
There are the Shoe Repair, the yellow dyers,
Dry Cleaning, and the Handy Mending Service,

---

630 **I brought . . . dowry** under Roman law divorce was easy
but involved the return of the wife's dowry to her; often this
was impossible, and so the wife had a perpetual hold over her
husband

Belt Makers, and the Custom Corsetry;   650
You think you've paid them off, they disappear,
Then come three hundred more to haunt the doorstep
With beggar's bags—the little milliners,
The men who make those fancy trinket boxes—
They go in for the handout. When you think you've paid
    them off,
In march the Golden Dying Specialists, Incorporated.
There's always some damned fellow wanting something.

    EUC. [*aside*] I'd break in, but I'm scared I'll interrupt
His speech on women's ways. I'll let him be.

    MEG. And when you've settled every last fool bill   660
There at the line's end comes a soldier, begging.
You run to check your bank account, the veteran
Waits, getting hungrier, expecting a donation;
And when you've finished arguing with your banker
You find you've run yourself an overdraft,
And so the soldier has cold hope for supper.
These are the annoyances, and many more besides,
The grinding extravagances that accompany large dowries.
A wife without a dowry is beneath her husband's thumb.
Those that possess them bring their menfolk nothing else   670
But bankruptcy and trouble. Isn't that my neighbor
Waiting on his doorstep? Euclio, how are you?

    EUC. I fairly ate up those remarks of yours.

    MEG. Oh, listening, were you?

    EUC.   Didn't miss a word.

    MEG. Well, frankly, you'd have better spent your time
In dressing up to see your daughter married.

    EUC. Those who dress up to their circumstances
And only make the show they can afford
Keep themselves mindful of their origins.
No, Megadorus. Neither I nor any poor man   680
Ever lived better for what people thought of him.

    MEG. You have sufficient. May the gods continue it,
And ever grant you increase of what you now possess.

    EUC. [*aside*] Hey! I don't like that "what you now
    possess!"
He knows what I've got here as well as I do.
The old girl told him everything.

    MEG. Hey! Are you holding a caucus with yourself?

    EUC. I'm figuring how to tell you what I think of you.

MEG. What?

EUC.　　　　　You're asking me, when you've filled every
　corner

690 Of my house with robbers? I was mortified!
When you sent five hundred cooks into my house
And every man of them six handed, like Geryon?
If Argus watched them, yes, the one who was all eyes,
The one that Juno set as Io's watchdog,
They'd even get past him—and not content with that,
A flute-girl—I ask you!—who could drink
The fountain of Pirene dry at Corinth
If it were running wine, all by herself!
And then the food—

MEG.　　　　　Enough to feed a regiment!
I even sent a lamb!

700 EUC.　　　　Oh yes, that lamb!
It was the most religious beast I'd ever seen!

MEG. You said religious?

EUC.　　　　　　　　Yes, it had been fasting—
There was nothing there but skin and bone.
You didn't have to kill the beast to read its guts,
Just stand it up against the light. It was transparent
As a paper lantern.

MEG.　　　　Why, I picked it out
For slaughtering myself.

EUC.　　　　　Then the best thing you can do
Is find an undertaker quick. It's on its last legs now.

MEG. [recovering his temper] Come on, Euclio, let's
　have a drink or two!

EUC. I wouldn't care to, thank you.

710 MEG.　　　　　Oh, come on! I'll have them.
Send over a good vintage from my cellar.

EUC. I said no thank you! I'm a firm teetotaler.

MEG. I'll get you drunk if there's a breath left in my
　body,
You old teetotaler!

692 **Geryon** fabulous triple-bodied monster defeated by Heracles　693-4 **Io** a river nymph seduced by Jupiter. Juno, his wife,
had her guarded by the monster **Argus**, variously depicted as
having three, four or many more eyes　697 **Pirene** famous fountain and landmark at Corinth, used both for water and as a
meeting place, richly decorated by successive benefactors

EUC. [*aside*]   I know exactly what he's thinking—
How he can get me drunk and leave me flat,
So *this* [*fondling his pot*] can have a change of scenery.
I'll watch for that! I'll hide it outdoors somewhere.
He'll waste his time and wine too, that's for sure.
    MEG. Well, if there's nothing I can do for you,
I'll go and scrub up for the sacrifice. [*Exit into his house.*]   720
    EUC. Dear me, you have a lot of enemies, old pot,
You and that gold I entrusted to your keeping.
The best thing I can do with you is take you
To the shrine of Faith, so I can hide you properly.
You know me, Faith, and I know you. Take care
You don't change your name, if I trust this to you.
Faith, here I come, relying on your faithfulness.

[*Exit* EUCLIO *to the shrine of Faith. Enter* STROBILUS.]

    STROBILUS. This is what a careful slave should do,
Follow my footsteps, and not look on master's orders
As a tiresome nuisance. No. A slave who claims   730
To serve his master as he wishes should put master first,
His own occasions second, and he should remember
That he's a servant even while he sleeps.
If he serves a master who's in love, as I do,
And sees he's passion's plaything, I advise him do as
        follows:
Bring him to his senses, and not push him where
His inclinations lead him—like boys who learn to swim;
You fit them with waterwings to make it easier,
So they can learn the strokes without much trouble.
And equally I think the slave should be his master's water-
        wings,   740
When he's in love, to hold him up from plummeting
Plop to the bottom, like a sinker. Let him
Study his master's authority, so he
Can tell his feelings at a glance, and carry out his orders
Faster than a four-horse chariot express.
With care, he'll never know the whip's sharp tongue
Or have to spend time polishing his fetters.
My master, now: he loves that poor old Euclio's daughter.
He's just got word she'll marry Megadorus.
He sent me as observer so he'll know what's going on.   750
I'll sit here on this altar, and they won't suspect a thing,

And snoop both ways, to see what's happening.

[*Enter* EUCLIO *from the shrine.*]

EUC. Now, Faith, don't tell a soul about my gold.
I'm not afraid they'll find it, it's been beautifully hidden
In the dark; but by heaven, if anybody did,
He'd have a fine haul there, a pot crammed full of gold.
And so I ask you, Faith, don't let them do it.
Now I'll go wash for holy service, so
I won't delay my neighbour one second from marrying
760 My daughter. Faith, you keep an eye on things.
When I come back for the pot, I want to see it as I left it.
I trust it to your honesty, it's in your home, your
    shrine . . .

[*Exit* EUCLIO *into his house.* STROBILUS *leaves his place at
        the altar.*]

STROB. Gods almighty, what did I hear that man saying?
He hid a pot of gold here, in the shrine of Faith?
Faith, don't be more faithful to him than to me.
I bet this is the father of the girl my master loves.
I'll look the temple over, to see if I can find
The gold while he's busy. But, O Faith! if I find it
I'll give you a gallon crock brimful of honeywine,
770 I will, I will, and drink it all myself!

[*Exit* STROBLUS *into the shrine. Enter* EUCLIO *from his
        house.*]

EUC. A crow cawed on my left. That means bad news.
He stood there scratching at the ground and croaking,
And all at once my heart did acrobatics
And bounded in my breast. But I must run!

[*He runs into the shrine, and immediately reappears,
        dragging* STROBILUS *after him.*]

Come out, you worm! Just crawled out of your hole, eh?
You didn't show yourself a minute ago.
But now you're here, I'll make you pay for it!
You crook, you'll wish you never had been born!
STROB. What the hell's got into you? Hey, old man,
780 What's the story? Why are you hitting me
This way? Where are you taking me?

What am I being beaten for?

EUC.   I'd like to beat you
To a jelly—are you asking me, you thief?
No, you're three thieves in one!

STROB.   What have I stolen?

EUC.   Give it back.

STROB. Give what back?

EUC.   Do you really need to ask?

STROB. Did you have something stolen?

EUC.   No, but you
Have something stolen, and I want it back!
Come on!

STROB. Come where?

EUC.   You'll never get away with it.

STROB. Well, what was it you wanted?

EUC.   Do you think I'm going
To take this lying down?

STROB. [*sniggering*]   It wouldn't be   790
The first thing that you've taken lying down.

EUC. Now cut the repartee, and hand it over!

STROB.   Hand what over?
You might at least give it a name.
I haven't taken anything of yours,
Or touched a thing.

EUC.   Come on, let's see your hands.

STROB. See, there they are.

EUC.   Hm. Where's the other one?

STROB. The old boy's nuts, he's gone stark raving mad.
This is no way to treat me.

EUC.   No, you're right,
I should have strung you up. And I will, too,
If you don't come clean

STROB.   Clean about what?   800

EUC. What have you stolen?

STROB.   Nothing, as I hope to die.
It never even crossed my mind.

EUC.   Come on shake out your cloak.

STROB. [*doing so*] You're the boss.

EUC.   It must be in your underclothes.

STROB. All right, then, search me.

EUC. [*doing so*]   Damned obliging, aren't you,
To make me think you haven't taken anything.

I'm wise to you. Let's start again. Hold out
Your right hand.

STROB. [*doing so*] There.

EUC.   The left one.

STROB. [*holding out both*]   Both at once.

EUC. [*struggling to be amiable*] All right, I give up.
Give it back.

STROB.   Give what back?

EUC. You're fooling, I know you've got it.

STROB.   Oh, I have?
Got what?

810   EUC.   You're only trying to make me tell.
But I won't. It doesn't matter what it is.
Give it back.

STROB.   You're nuts. I gave you a free hand
To search me, and you didn't find a thing.

EUC. Hey, wait! Who was with you? There must have
been
Somebody else in there, some other man . . .
Oh, this is awful! He's inside there now, and if I
Take my eyes off this one I'll have lost him.
But then, I've searched him and he's clean.
[*to* STROBILUS]   Get out.

STROB. I hope you rot in hell.

EUC. [*aside*]   He has a pretty way
820 Of saying thank you. [*to* STROBILUS] Now I'll go in, and get
My hands around the throat of your accomplice.
Out of my sight! Well, are you getting out of here
Or aren't you?

STROB.   Yes, I'm going.

EUC. And if ever I set eyes on you again . . . [*Exit to
the shrine.*]

STROB. I hope I die a horrible death, if I
Don't make a fool of that old man today.
He won't dare hide the gold there any longer—
I guess he'll take it with him, and change places.

[EUCLIO *emerges from the shrine, carrying the pot of gold.*]

Hey, that's the door. And there's the old boy bringing
830 His gold outside. I'll stand behind the door a bit.

[STROBILUS *conceals himself, while* EUCLIO *addresses the
shrine.*]

EUC. I thought if anyone were faithful it would be
Faith there—and then she nearly made a monkey of me!
If that crow hadn't come to my assistance
So help me, I'd be ruined. I'd be glad to see
That crow again, the one who tipped me off,
So I could give him a good word—for if I
Gave him food, he'd only eat it. Now I wonder
Where I can find some solitary place
To hide my gold? There's a grove outside the walls
Sacred to Silvanus, with a thick stand of willow.   840
No one ever goes there. It'll suit me fine.
And I know one thing—I can trust Silvanus
A whole lot further than I trust in Faith. [*Exit.*]
    STROB. [*coming from hiding*] Great! Wonderful! Some-
        one up there likes me.
I'll run ahead of him and climb a tree
And watch where the old boy's burying his gold.
Master ordered me to wait here—but who cares?
I know one thing, if I'm in trouble anyway
I might as well make money out of it.

[*Exit* STROBILUS *following* EUCLIO. *Enter* LYCONIDES *and*
                    EUNOMIA.]

    LYCONIDES. Well, mother, that's the story. Now you
        know as much as I do   850
About me and Euclio's daughter. Now I beg you, mother,
And entreat you, do what I begged you to before,
Mention the matter to my uncle, mother.
    EUN. You know I wish you all you wish yourself.
I'm confident that I can make my brother promise—
And it's only fair, if your story's really true,
That you got drunk, and raped an honest girl.
    LYC. Mother, could I look you in the face and lie?
    PHAEDRIA. [*offstage, inside* EUCLIO'*s house*]. Nurse, I
        can't stand it!
Help, the pains are starting!
Our lady of childbirth, save me!
    LYC.   Mother, perhaps   860
You'll believe that! How she cries, the baby's coming!
    EUN. Son, come along with me to see my brother,

840 **Silvanus** rustic deity with power over uncultivated land

So I can get from him the favor that you wanted.
  LYC. I'll be with you in a moment.

[*Exit* EUNOMIA *to* MEGADORUS' *house*.]

                     But I wonder where
My slave has got to? I gave strict instructions
He was to wait here for me. But on second thoughts
If he's on my business, it's not fair to bawl him out.
[*turning toward* MEGADORUS' *house*]
Well, in we go, to face the jury. [*Exit*.]

[*Enter* STROBILUS.]

  STROB. [*clutching the pot*] I'm richer now than any
    leprechaun
870 All by my little self—and as for all those
Other monarchs, they aren't worth a mention,
Poor beggars! I'm His Majesty King Philip.
Oh happy day! When I left here just now
I got there long before he did, and settled myself
In a tree. I sat there waiting till I saw
Where the old man hid his gold. When he was gone
"Come on," I told myself, shinned down the tree,
Dug up the pot of gold. While I was there
I saw the old man coming back again.
880 He didn't see me, though; I took a detour.
Hahah! Here he comes! I'll go hide this at home.

[*Exit* STROBILUS. *Enter* EUCLIO, *running wildly*.]

  EUC. Death, murder, destruction! Which way shall I run
Or not run? Stop thief! Stop what thief?
What's his name? I've no idea,
I'm in a fog, I'm running blind.
I haven't any clear idea of where
I'm going, who I am or what my name is.
[*to the audience*]
I beg, I pray you, I beseech you, come
To my assistance, tell me where he went,
890 The man who stole it—You, sir, what do you say?
I'm sure you can be trusted; you have an honest face.
What is it? What's so funny? I know your lot—
Crooks, that's what you are, ninety-nine percent of you.

You sit in whitewashed togas, and pretend
That you're respectable—doesn't anyone here have it?
You don't know? Murder! Then tell me who does!
Don't you know anything?

Misery, misery, I'm destroyed,
Wiped out, in sackcloth and ashes.
This day has brought me such weeping and sorrow,   900
Agony, bankruptcy and starvation
I'm the world's greatest expert on them.
What do I have to live for, now
I've lost the gold I'd so carefully hidden?
I've cheated myself, my hopes, my dreams,
And everybody will laugh to see me
Take it so hard—I can't endure it!

[*Enter* LYCONIDES *from* MEGADORUS' *house.*]

LYC. Who's making such a racket, and crying at the
   door?
I guess that must be Euclio; I'm done, the secret's out.
He knows his daughter's had a baby. Now the question   910
Is, shall I go or face him? Stay or run? I wish I knew.
EUC. Who's talking?
LYC.   I am, more's the pity.
EUC.   No,
I need the pity. I'm in such pitiful plight,
Such trouble, so unhappy—
LYC.   Keep your spirits up.
EUC. And how do you expect me to do that?
LYC.   This thing
That's so upset you—I confess I did it.
EUC.   What?
What did you say?
LYC.   The truth.
EUC.   What have I ever
Done to you, young man, that you should treat me so?
And ruin me and my children?
LYC.   It was the devil in me,
Putting temptation in my way.
EUC.   Explain yourself.   920
LYC. I see the error of my ways, and know I should be
   censured,

And so I've come to ask you to be patient and forgive me.

EUC. How dare you lay a finger on someone else's property?

LYC. What do you expect? It's done, and nothing can
undo it now.

I think it must be fated, or it never would have happened.

EUC. I think it must be fated that I take you home and
flog you!

LYC. No, don't say that!

EUC.　　　　　　　　What do you mean by laying

Hands on my treasure without my permission?

LYC. Blame love and wine.

EUC.　　　　　　　　I never heard such impudence!

930 You have a nerve, to stand there and say that to my face!

If you're allowed to go without your punishment

What's there to stop us snatching purses in broad daylight?

If we're arrested, we'll say "Sorry, we were drunk!

Lay the blame on love!" Love, wine, they're trashy things

If the drunkard and the lover can get away with murder.

LYC. But I've come freely to ask pardon for my foolish-
ness.

EUC. I don't like people who do something wrong, and
then

Go around whining that they didn't mean it.

You knew you had no right—you should have kept your
hands off!

LYC. All right. But given that I haven't kept my hands

940 off,

I won't beat about the bush. I say that finding's keepings.

EUC. Over my dead body!

LYC.　　　　　　　　No, I don't ask that;

I'm only asking for my rights. I think you'll find

I have a better claim than anybody, Euclio.

EUC. If you don't give it back I'll march you off to court

And sue you—

LYC.　　　　Give what back?

EUC.　　　　　　　　My stolen property.

LYC. I stole your property? Where from? What is it?

EUC. Lord bless the boy. As if you didn't know.

LYC.　　　　　　　　How can I

Unless you tell me what you're looking for?

EUC. My pot of gold, that's what I'm asking for;   950
You admitted it already.

LYC.   I said no such thing!
I never touched it!

EUC.   You deny it?

LYC.   Certainly.
I don't know anything about your gold
Or pot, for that matter.

EUC.   The pot you stole
From the grove of Silvanus! Give it back, come on;
Hand it over. I'll go shares, I'll give you half.
You're a crook, but I won't argue, honest. Give it back.

LYC. You must be crazy calling me a thief.
I thought that you'd discovered something else
I have an interest in—a thing of great importance   960
I must talk over with you at your leisure, Euclio.

EUC. On your honor, now. You didn't steal my gold?

LYC. No, on my honor.

EUC.   You don't know who did?

LYC. Nor that, on my honor.

EUC.   If you did find out
You'd tell me?

LYC.   Certainly.

EUC.   You wouldn't cover up
For him, and share the proceeds?

LYC.   No, of course not.

EUC. And if you break your promise?

LYC.   Then may I be dealt with
As god above sees fit.

EUC.   That's fair enough.
Now, what's on your mind?

LYC.   In case you aren't
Acquainted with my family, my uncle's Megadorus,   970
My father was Antimachus, my name's Lyconides,
Eunomia's my mother.

EUC.   Now I know your family,
What's your problem? That's what I should like to know.

LYC. You have a daughter.

EUC.   She's at home right now.

LYC. I understand that you've engaged her to my uncle.

EUC.   Quite correct.

LYC. He asked me to tell you the engagement's off.

EUC. Off? When everything's ready? When she's bought
her trousseau?

Oh, you immortal gods and goddesses,

Blast him to little pieces; I've wasted

980 A fortune all because of him today.

LYC. Don't fret, and take that back. Pray rather

For fortune and good health, for you and for your daughter.

Come on, say it.

EUC. [unwillingly] Bless us both.

LYC.   And me as well. Now listen.

There isn't any man so cheap that when

He knows that he's done something wrong

He doesn't feel ashamed and try to clear himself.

I beg you, Euclio, with all my heart,

If I've committed any injury unknowingly

Against you or your daughter, pardon me

990 And let me marry her as law requires.

I might as well own up. At the watchnight feast of Ceres

When I was drunk and swept away by youthful

Exuberance—I wronged your daughter.

EUC.   Eh?

You did what, you say?

LYC.   What are you shouting at?

I've made you a grandad for your daughter's wedding!

Your daughter's had a baby—nine months—work it out.

That's why my uncle broke it off, for my sake;

Go in, and see if things aren't as I say.

EUC.   My life's in pieces!

So many troubles coming all together . . .

I'll go inside and get the truth of it. [Exit to his house.]

1000 LYC.   I'll follow.

It looks as if we'll soon be on firm ground again.

I wish I knew where that Strobilus has disappeared to.

Well, I can wait a bit and go in later.

I'll give him time to crossexamine the old woman

Who runs attendance on his daughter; she knows everything.

[Enter STROBILUS. He fails to see LYCONIDES at first.]

STROB. O you immortal gods, what weight of pure
  delight
You bestow on me; this pot, four pounds
Of solid gold, is mine, all mine. Can anyone
Beat that? Is there another man in Athens
Who stands in heaven's favor more than I do now?   1010
  LYC. I'm sure I heard somebody talking here just now.
  STROB. [seeing LYCONIDES] Hey! Is that my master?
  LYC. [seeing STROBILUS]   Is that man my slave?
  STROB. [aside] Himself.
  LYC. [aside]   That's him all right.
  STROB. [aside]   Here goes.
  LYC. [aside]   I'll go and meet him.
I dare say he's done what I told him to
And gone to the old woman, the young lady's nurse.
  STROB. Why don't I let him in on it, and admit
I found the treasure? I can ask him for my freedom.
I'll get it off my chest. [to LYCONIDES] I've found—
  LYC.   Found what?
  STROB. Not chicken-feed, sir!
  LYC.   There you go again.
You're never serious.
  STROB.   No, I'll tell you, master: 1020
Wait till you hear this.
  LYC.   Go ahead, I'm listening.
  STROB. Today I found a fortune.
  LYC.   Where?
  STROB.   A four pound pot,
I tell you, full of gold.
  LYC.   You found a what?
  STROB. I stole it from old Euclio.
  LYC.   Where is this gold?
  STROB. Home, in my box. I'd like to ask you for my
  freedom.
  LYC. You're asking me to set you free,
You mountain of iniquity?
  STROB. Hands off, master. I know what you're up to.
I really made you prick your ears up, didn't I?
[trying to pass it off as a joke]
You were all set to take it off my hands.   1030
What would you do if I'd really found it?

LYC. You can't fool me. Come on.
Hand over the gold.
    STROB.   Me? Hand it over?
    LYC. That's what I said, so he can have it back.
    STROB. Now where would I get gold?
    LYC.   Why, you just said
You put it in your box.
    STROB.   You know the way I talk—
It doesn't mean a thing.
    LYC.   You give it back or else—
    STROB. Over my dead body!

[*At this point the original text breaks off.*]

    LYC. [*striking him*]   With the greatest pleasure!
    STROB. No, wait, Lyconides! It isn't fair
1040 That I should put myself to so much trouble
To find the gold and then get nothing for it.
So let's make things easier for both of us:
Give me my freedom, and I'll give you the gold.
    LYC. No promises until I see the gold.

[*Enter* EUCLIO *from his house, driving* STAPHYLA *before him.*]

But here comes Euclio. Let's go fetch it quickly;
I'd hate to see him do himself a mischief.

[*Exeunt.*]

    EUC. [*to* STAPHYLA] Out of my house, you interfering witch,
You snake-in-the-grass, you liar! You can go starve
For all I care! Do you think I'm going to keep you
1050 In my house another minute, when you've made
A fool of me for nine months put together?
I never want to see your face again.
Count yourself lucky I don't strangle you.

[*Enter* MEGADORUS *from his house.*]

    MEG. Hey, Euclio, what's the matter now? Don't hurt her.
    EUC. You think perhaps I owe her a reward
For fooling me this way? As for my daughter

As soon as she gets on her feet again
Out she goes too.
    MEG.   Now keep your temper, Euclio.
I know just how you feel, and in a way
It does you credit. But they've done no harm.   1060
    EUC. Oh yes, it's all very well for you to say so,
Megadorus. But I've had enough of you
And all your family. Because you're rich
You think you can treat me any way you fancy.
First you come sneaking up to me and say
"Please may I marry your daughter?" When
You've talked me into it against my better judgment
You turn around and say "I've changed my mind;
I'm going to pass her to my nephew." And as if that
    weren't enough
It turns out she was pregnant, and that all this while   1070
Here I've been living in a fool's paradise.
And on top of that, the treasure that I loved,
My precious pot of gold's been stolen from me.
By all the gods, I wish I never had been born.
    MEG. Now don't take on so. When I asked to marry
    her
I was speaking honestly. I admired her
And still do. But my nephew's claim
Takes precedence. I give her up unwillingly;
But he's in love with her. I know he'll make
A splendid husband for her, Euclio,   1080
And one who has more life left in him
Than I have. Give them both your blessing.
    ECU. You want me to give my daughter to a drunkard,
A seducer? No! I'd rather kill her first.

       [*Enter* LYCONIDES *with the pot of gold.*]

But here he comes. [*turning his back*] I've nothing more
    to say to him.
    LYC. Euclio, don't turn your back on me, although
I well deserve it. Here's a little something
That might well cause you to think better of me.
    EUC. I'm not interested in anything that you could give
    me.
    LYC. [*showing the pot*] Not even this?
    EUC.   He's found my pot of gold! 1090

LYC. I'll let you have it on one condition, Euclio:
Give me your daughter. Let's be friends again.

EUC. Oh, very well. There seems to be some good in you
After all.

MEG. Now listen to me, Euclio.
Now that you're thinking better of us, and I'm one
Of the family, so to speak, I'm going to give you
A bit of good advice. This pot of gold:
What good has it ever done you since you had it?
You've been a different man, suspecting everyone,

1100 Jumpy, bad-tempered. Hoarding money
Never did anybody any good.
It's only useful when it's put to use.
So my advice to you is this:
Give it away and get it off your mind.

EUC. You're asking me to give away my gold?

MEG. To those you love—your daughter and Lyconides.

EUC. I hardly like to say it, but I think you're right.
Since I discovered it, I've never had
A minute's peace, day or night; I'll get some sleep now

1110 If I get rid of it. All right, then.
I'll give it to my daughter as a dowry.

MEG. No, not your daughter. Remember what I said
Before? She's a good girl, don't go spoiling her
With money. As for Lyconides,
He doesn't need it, all my money's his.
So give it as a present to your grandson
And I'll keep it in trust for him until he needs it.
When he's of an age to be extravagant
He'll never need to borrow from his father.

1120 EUC. All right, then take it; but whatever you do
Never let me set eyes on it again
Or I might change my mind.

MEG.   No, I don't think so.
A carefree heart is worth a mint of money.
Now come in to dinner, every one
To celebrate the wedding of Lyconides!

EUC. [*to the audience*] And you, spectators, give us
  your applause.

BIBLIOGRAPHY

BIBLIOGRAPHY

THE ANCIENT THEATRE

Arnott, P. D., *An Introduction to the Greek Theatre* (Bloomington: Indiana University Press, 1963).

Beare, W., *The Roman Stage* (London, Methuen, 1950).

Bieber, M., *The History of the Greek and Roman Theater*, second edition (Princeton, N.J.: Princeton University Press, 1961).

Flickinger, R. C., *The Greek Theater and its Drama*. Chicago: Chicago University Press, 1936.

TEXTS AND TRANSLATIONS

Aristophanes, *Comedies*, ed. F. W. Hall and W. M. Geldart, 2 vols. (Oxford: The Clarendon Press, 1906). Greek text with critical apparatus.

Aristophanes, *Comedies*, ed. B. B. Rogers, 11 vols. (London: G. Bell and Sons, 1907-30). Greek text, extensive commentary and facing verse translation.

Plautus, *Comedies*, ed. W. M. Lindsay, 2 vols. (Oxford: The Clarendon Press, 1908.) Latin text with critical apparatus.

Plautus, *Comedies*, trans. P. Nixon, Loeb Classical Library, 5 vols. (New York and Harvard (Vol. 5) 1916-1951). Latin text with facing English translation.

The Complete Roman Drama, ed. G. E. Duckworth, 2 vols. (New York: Random House, 1942). Translations from various sources.

ANALYSIS AND CRITICISM

Cornford, F. M., *The Origin of Attic Comedy* (New York: Doubleday, 1961).

Duckworth, G. E., *The Nature of Roman Comedy: a study in popular entertainment* (Princeton, N.J.: Princeton University Press, 1952).

Lever, K., *The Art of Greek Comedy* (London: Methuen, 1956).

Murray, G., *Aristophanes* (Oxford: The Clarendon Press, 1933).

Norwood, G., *Greek Comedy* (London: Methuen, 1931).

Of various individual translations, those by Dudley Fitts (*Birds, Frogs, Lysistrata*) and the Complete Greek Comedies series published by the University of Michigan Press are worth attention for their stimulating critical comments on the plays.